Hidden
CANADA

AN
intimate
TRAVELOGUE

Norman Ravvin

Red Deer Press

The Publishers
Red Deer Press
813 MacKimmie Library Tower
2500 University Drive N.W.
Calgary Alberta Canada T2N 1N4

Credits
Cover photograph by Bill Frymire/Masterfile
Cover design by Duncan Campbell
Text design by Dennis Johnson
Printed and bound in Canada by Friesens for Red Deer Press

Acknowledgements
Financial support provided by the Canada Council, the Department of Canadian Heritage, the Alberta Foundation for the Arts, a beneficiary of the Lottery Fund of the Government of Canada, and the University of Calgary.

National Library of Canada Cataloguing in Publication Data
Ravvin, Norman, 1963–
Hidden Canada
ISBN 0-88995-226-4
1. Ravvin, Norman, 1963– —Journeys—Canada.
2. Canada—Description and travel. I. Title.
FC75.R38 2001   917.104′648   C00-911057-7
F1017.R38 2001

5   4   3   2   1

Photography Acknowledgements

All photos by Norman Ravvin except as noted.

*The Publishers gratefully acknowledge the following for
permission to reprint images appearing in this book:*

Special Collections, University Archives Division,
University of British Columbia Library,
Malcolm Lowry Collection, BC1614/260, page 53

Watercolour by Edward John Hughes, Calgary, Canada, 1956,
Glenbow Collection, Calgary, Canada, page 76

The Fee House, watercolour by Michael Kluckner, 1989, page 152

For my father, who knew the pleasures of the road.

What is that feeling when you're driving away from people and they recede on the plain till you see their specks dispersing?—it's the too-huge world vaulting us, and it's good-by. But we lean forward to the next crazy venture beneath the skies.

–JACK KEROUAC

Contents

Hidden

CANADA

AN
intimate
TRAVELOGUE

Introduction

ONE OF THE BEST—and too little known—travel books portraying Canada is Edward Hoagland's *Notes From the Century Before.* With the let-things-come-as-they-may attitude of a beat hobo or a circus roustabout, Hoagland travels by boat and seaplane into the northernmost reaches of British Columbia, a landscape that had boomed with the Klondike Gold Rush. But by 1966, when Hoagland chronicled it, northern British Columbia had slipped back into a state of semiwildness, becoming a territory full of aging mountain men, failed schemes, the odd American big-game hunter and the dwindling towns of the Tahltan and Tagish tribes. At times Hoagland seems a bit embarrassed by his project, as if his travels into this largely unknown landscape represent a kind of madness, the folly of a young, melancholic man at loose ends. While surveying an isolated town, he wonders,

> And why am I so elated? Am I an antiquarian? It all adds up to whatever you make of it. I'm elated because I respond as I did on my first ocean voyage. It's as though the last bit of ocean were about to become more dry land, planted and paved. The loss would not be to us who have already sailed it. . . . The loss is to people unborn who might have turned into seamen, or who might have seen it and loved it as we, alive now and not seamen, have seen it and loved it.

Hoagland is haunted by the sense that things in northern British Columbia are on the verge of great change, that the men and women he is visiting will soon be swept from the scene. One curious aspect of his approach to his subject is his lack of interest in how it fits into the larger Canadian scene. He is a lover of the particular places he visits, a collector of the voices found there, but he is a New York City writer with no journalistic interest in Canada's transformation at the high point of its postwar prosperity.

Another grand book of ramblings in Canada is Norman Levine's *Canada Made Me.* An Ottawa-born fiction writer, Levine has lived much of his adult life abroad, and, in fact, he wrote *Canada Made Me* as part of a long visit to his native country, viewing it from the perspective of self-imposed exile. In much of his travels, Levine is downbeat and even surly about the places he visits. Unlike Hoagland, he is not interested in the pace of change, in the North American habit of remaking things each generation. Instead, he views his homeland the way an Englishman might see his native countryside—as tradition-bound, enervated, unreflective. But like Hoagland, Levine is compelled by the details of daily life that are strange and surprising—a fisherman's progress on his boat near Tofino or a hotelkeeper's stinginess in small-town New Brunswick. Levine's is the poet's love of momentary flashes of beauty in everyday life.

In these essays of the place I call Hidden Canada, I pursue some of these same flashes, underwritten by the melancholy sense of loss and wonder that comes with an awareness of change sweeping away communities and ways of life before it.

Unlike Hoagland and Levine, I view Canada from the point of view of an insider. Born in Calgary, I've lived in Vancouver, Toronto, Fredericton and Montréal. But I share with Hoagland the sense of elation that can come with a visit to a place entirely unknown and unlike anything experienced before. Hoagland, waking up in the town of Telegraph Creek on a dazzling June morning, says it is "like having a second language to be at home here. I'm a different personality." Telegraph Creek's ability to transform its visitor comes of its separateness from the

North American mainstream, from its ability to harbour human types, a plentitude of wildlife and ways of communal living that are part of another era. To emphasize these discoveries, Hoagland gives his portrait of 1960s British Columbia the paradoxical title *Notes From the Century Before,* which signals that he has gone looking for the past of Northern Canada even as he records its inevitable disappearance. He tries to put his hand on what remains and capture the voices bridging the gap between a hidden past and today. In Hoagland's case, as with the essays collected here in *Hidden Canada,* this kind of investigation is a labour of the heart.

In recounting my travels across the country, I have tried to recover layers of the past that have been swept away in Canadian cities and rural places. In this country the past goes to the wrecking ball, to the city council vote, to the ratepayers' demand that an eyesore be tidied up so it won't affect property values. The Canadian past is too often made to go away quietly without a struggle. Few bother to record what is lost, and few markers are set up to remind us of what stood on a site first, next and last, before the present skyscraper or glittering home. One of the oddest aspects of this phenomenon is the party atmosphere—complete with deck chairs, beer and New Year's Day–like hurrahs—when a substantial old building is dynamited.

IN EACH OF THE FOLLOWING CHAPTERS, my goal is to make the past of a site present to the reader and to visitors who might find their way there. I've chosen places where the amazing pace of change, the transformation in the course of a century or two, is most remarkable. Calgary's downtown is an obvious subject, ripe for excavation. But so too is the complicated and changing history of the south shore of the St. Lawrence, across from Montréal, where, nestled in the shadow of the Mercier Bridge, the Mohawk town of Kahnawake struggles to find contemporary meaning in an icon of the past. In another chapter I go in search of the layers of history hidden on the farm land of southwestern Ontario, where fugitive blacks made their homes before the abolition of slavery in the American South. The oldest site I visit is Trinity, Newfoundland, where the past still sits heavy on a town that seems to have bet its future on efforts at repackaging heritage as an enticement for tourists. Among the landscapes of this country where the past has been most completely effaced is the North Shore of Vancouver's Burrard Inlet, where a famous writer lived and wrote influential books that make no mention at all of the centuries of Squamish history predating the squatter society on the coastal flats. Two other chapters focus on the transformations undergone by Canadian urban and rural society in the last one hundred years: in Vancouver's West End, a varied bohemian lifestyle has given way to an irrefutable fact, possibly our new god: soaring real estate values. In southern Saskatchewan, the opposite phenomenon—a devaluing and depeopling of the landscape—leaves only the barest ghostly markers of the unusual farming settlements that once existed just north of the American border.

THE PARTICULARITY OF CANADIANS' RELATIONSHIP to their past came home to me on a recent trip to Warsaw, which, oddly enough, made me think about the city where I grew up. Calgary is known outside Canada as a tourist destination because of the winter Olympics held there in 1988 and because of its proximity to the Rocky Mountains and Banff. But part of its reputation abroad also has to do with its nearly complete demolition of architecture dating from before 1960. No other city, it is said, pulled down so much of its early buildings in order to make way for boom-time construction. Some architects were interested in this fact, but for most Calgarians things were simply moving forward as they had since the city's beginnings in the 1880s. Recently, preservation has come into vogue as it has in the rest of Canada. Old banks and even the main floor of the building that once housed the original Burns slaughterhouse have become upscale restaurants. But what remains after all the demolition is a few impressive sandstone buildings, the odd church in the shadow of glass high-rises and a sprinkling of the city's characteristic seventy-year-old wood-frame houses—barely enough for visitors to be able to picture what Calgary looked like in 1950, let alone 1920.

Upon visiting Poland, I discovered that Warsaw is in fact Calgary's opposite when it comes to architectural history. The seven-hundred-year-old capital by the banks of the Vistula was almost completely destroyed under German occupation during the Second World War. In response to the uprising in the Jewish ghetto and the revolt of the Polish Home Army, the Germans simply destroyed the city, blowing up one neighbourhood after the next as they cleared the ancient apartment blocks of rebel fighters and citizens in hiding. Photos of Warsaw after the German retreat show a city of rubble, block after block of paving stones, exploded masonry, monuments broken into pieces. Almost as quickly as the Germans were gone, the Poles began propping up the few façades that had survived the carnage in the hope that they might be saved. In this instinctive impulse toward preservation was the beginning of an amazing post-war project: the reconstruction of large parts of the city in the image of its prewar self. Buildings erected in the eighteenth and nineteenth centuries were rebuilt using plans, photographs and drawings made by European visitors to Warsaw. Today, a typical plaque on a downtown building reads, "Built before 1733. Destroyed 1939. Rebuilt 1950." The Old Town, Warsaw's medieval centre, was completely and minutely recreated. Its streets—with their elaborate gabled houses, ripely painted royal palaces and numerous commemorative plaques and statues—fool the eye of any visitor into thinking that it is an eastern Prague or Paris, a jewel of ancient architectural heritage, when in fact, post-war city planners erected nearly everything "old" in an effort to deny the Germans' project of destroying Warsaw's past.

In contrast with this consider Calgary, a Canadian boom town at the confluence of the Bow and Elbow rivers, being patiently being taken down by its own citizens, the tracks of its past covered so completely that it might be thought that there were none. So much of Calgary's history has vanished that the city presents itself as a kind of Western Oz, a miraculous modern pot of gold at the end of a rainbow of oil money.

I try not to be sentimental in these portraits of Hidden Canada. What's gone is gone. At times I muse about how things might have been. And in each essay I try to put the reader in contact with what remains of a vanished way of life through the voices of people I met and descriptions of things on the ground that can still be touched. This is the resolutely upbeat aspect of my efforts to discover Hidden Canada, my guiding motive in fact: by recovering a sense of how lives were once lived in each landscape, we can come to know more than a shadow of the past and hear voices that point us backward without necessarily bemoaning what's lost. This may allow us to rebuild, at least in our minds, a kind of dream Canada, just as the Poles, in a more strenuous way, rebuilt Warsaw to exist as if it were never destroyed. I hope that for those who read of the places I visited, the picture created in the mind is sharp, textured and resonates with life. It may be too that the picture in the mind will provide a kind of map, a guide to some street corner or far-flung section of the countryside, where, like morning in Edward Hoagland's Telegraph Creek, a strangeness will somehow feel like home.

Kateri Tekakwitha

THE PRIEST CALLED ME from Kahnawake on a Tuesday afternoon. He'd written a week before to introduce himself, having found that I was teaching in Fredericton. His name was Louis Cyr, and as it turned out he'd be in my part of the country because it was his mother's ninety-fourth birthday. He'd grown up in New Brunswick but hadn't spent much time there since his youth, when his first assignments with the Jesuits had taken him elsewhere. He told me he'd seen a piece I'd written on Kahnawake in a Québec magazine. And he was sorry he'd missed me when I'd gone to visit the Mohawk reserve. At Kahnawake, on the south shore of the St. Lawrence, he ran the parish, with its old mission, whose centrepiece is a centuries-old grey stone church. The most unusual thing about the sanctuary of his church is that it houses the remains of Kateri Tekakwitha, a Mohawk in line to be sainted by the Vatican. Would I like to meet and talk, he asked, about what I'd written?

The day Louis Cyr came to see me was bright and warm for an hour or two in the midafternoon. I offered him coffee (he took tea), and we sat in my living room before a wall of windows as the day grew gradually colder and darker.

Louis Cyr was careful not to say he disagreed with what I'd written about the relationship between his church and Québec Mohawks. He seemed curious about me and about my fascination with Kateri

Tekakwitha. He said he knew some of the people I'd talked to. And the few he didn't, he was curious about. How did I meet so-and-so? When I told him, he seemed bemused and a bit flummoxed, as if a party had been thrown by friends of his who'd forgotten to invite him. There was so much he wanted to tell me about the reserve at Kahnawake, and as the afternoon wore on, it became clear that our conversation was underwritten by certain big unanswered questions concerning Canada: what its borders mean, whether struggles like that between the Jesuits and Mohawks should be looked into by outsiders, why anyone other than those intimate to this quarrel would be interested in the history of a young Mohawk woman bound for sainthood.

In fact, I had avoided meeting with the mission priest when I first visited Kahnawake, talking instead with people I met haphazardly as I wandered the shore of the seaway. I wanted to hear as much as I could from the Mohawks living on the reserve and as little as possible from everyone else: the government officials and priests and sociologists whose lives were entangled with the Mohawks but not quite a part of their community. Kahnawake is among the places in Canada where the country's deepest predicaments, its most indissoluble historical and social entanglements, make themselves clear. It is a town of eighty-seven hundred or so Mohawks on twelve thousand acres of reserve land across the seaway from Montréal. When you stand on the Kahnawake side of the river, across the wide, placid waters of the seaway from the green shoulder of Montréal's Mountain, you can make out the domes and towers of Catholic churches that dominate the city's neighbourhoods from the edge of Westmount to Old Montréal. Though Canada's second biggest city is just a short ride back over the Mercier Bridge, Kahnawake is a world apart, its grassy shoreline really a border Canada shares with another nation that exists in the imagination of many contemporary Mohawks. Since the first contact between the French and Mohawks in 1609, European and native residents along the river have remained as culturally remote from one another as two solitudes possibly can, even as they became increasingly entangled in transactions over land, trade and reli-

A street in Kahnawake, not far from the St. Lawrence Seaway

gious faith. This fact makes it difficult for most of us to see native Canada. It is hidden from us by a great gulf of mistrust. And, of course, so much of it is gone, destroyed by waves of settlement, by modernization and the steady whittling away of reserve land.

The most substantial marker of the troubled history of Kahnawake, which symbolizes both the intimate connections and mistrust between the French and Mohawk nations, is Louis Cyr's pastoral outpost—a grey stone church built in 1720 to house the Jesuit mission called St-François-Xavier. The church was built as part of the French fortress, Fort St. Louis, and it is the fourth appearance of a Jesuit mission along this stretch of the St. Lawrence—the first having been built in 1667, fifteen miles away at La Prairie. In the church's sanctuary, entombed within a great white block of Carrara marble, are the remains of Kateri Tekakwitha.

The historical record on Tekakwitha is thin. We know that she was born in 1656 at the Mohawk village of Ossernenon in New York State's Mohawk River Valley, forty miles west of what is now the state capital at Albany. Jesuits baptized Tekakwitha when she was twenty, after which she became a target of abuse in her community. She was smuggled north by canoe along trade routes to Kahnawake, which was known at the time as the Praying Village because of its reputedly devout community of Mohawk and Huron converts. Tekakwitha's faith became legendary through a number of Jesuit biographies written after her death, and cures and miraculous events became associated with her. Early in this century, Jesuits from New York State became involved in an effort to promote her as a candidate for sainthood, and in 1980 she was beatified by Pope John Paul II, this being the last step before she becomes the first native North American saint.

A visitor might well see the old stone church where Tekakwitha is entombed as a kind of crossing place, where the distance between the imaginative lives of the Mohawk people and those of French-speaking Catholics is overcome, a place where the most famous Mohawk in the world is commemorated while she waits for the utmost recognition from the Catholic Church. Once, the church might have represented a place where Indian Canada merged in a meaningful way with Canada's national culture, where the two nations recognized the extent of their entanglement. But if you stand in the parking lot today across from the church grounds and watch the school kids running home along streets of neat bungalows, some ducking into Porky's Pool Hall or hanging around out front of the Native Book Store, it seems that the old church is invisible to them, just another shadow thrown by the shifting light that fades and rises behind a slate-grey afternoon sky.

IN MANY WAYS, Kahnawake remains a riddle for natives to unlock on their own. Three centuries of lousy history were inflicted on the Mohawks by European traders, missionaries, and government agents, and in the minds of many of Kahnawake's residents, the drive to assimilate them into mainstream culture and expropriate their land has simply been inherited by the present provincial and federal governments. With this history it's difficult for a nonnative with no real connection to the place to get beyond the monologues about Québec–Mohawk relations that are

The Jesuit church at Kahnawake, also known as "Sanctuaire Kateri"

repeated in newspaper columns and government circles. These lines of information run like white noise above the real local dialogues, somehow convincing us that we understand Kahnawake's predicament, when in fact they do nothing more than complicate an already difficult situation. Just when a visitor begins to feel a certain confidence and sympathy with this history, someone will pause, in midconversation and ask, a little shyly, but with persistence, *What's brought you here?*

Part of Kateri's history is lodged far away from Kahnawake, across the Canada–U.S. border in the Mohawk River Valley in New York State. There, the Jesuit Brotherhood runs an elaborate shrine to Kateri Tekakwitha on magnificent, rolling countryside that was once the heart of Mohawk tribal territory. The shrine is near the town of Auriesville, on a hilltop where the palisaded village of Ossernenon stood before the arrival of French missionaries. I wandered the shrine's carefully landscaped grounds shortly before it opened for the summer season. I was alone but for a few pensive-looking pilgrims I saw in the shadow of a succession of ever-bigger churches built to commemorate Jesuit martyrs. I

The poles marking the once-palisaded Mohawk village are among a number of monuments at the Jesuit shrine to Kateri near Auriesville, New York

wondered if it occurred to them that there was almost nothing on the grounds that recalled the Mohawk civilization that had once flourished on these hills. The palisades—high wood post stockades that surrounded the village—are commemorated, but as part of a giant torture machine. Rough wooden poles meant to approximate the original posts bear hand-painted signs that read:

PALISADE
Marking the S.W. corner of Ossernenon
Mohawk Village where St. Isaac Joques and Rene Goupil were tortured, held captive and martyred 1642–46. Here St. John Lalande died 1646, and Katherine Tekakwitha was born, 1656. The heads of Joques and Lalande were impaled on one of the poles.

Images of Tekakwitha are everywhere—on post boards, carved in wood, in the stained glass of chapel windows through which visitors can

Iconic images of Kateri Tekakwitha often have the look of a Hollywood poster

watch the wobbly track of trucks on the New York Thruway. Not surprisingly, in all these portraits, the girl who would be saint looks anything but native. She could be Portuguese or Salvadorean or a Moroccan Jew for that matter, and artists never portray her as the wasting twenty-four-year-old she was when she died of something like consumption in the winter of 1680. Many of the shrine's images of Tekakwitha are reminiscent of the dusky Madonnas that cause a stir in Mexico and Poland; she appears before the Catholic faithful as a hail and handsome blanketed princess who, the Jesuits claim, carried her self-flagellation to extreme lengths in order to come as close as possible to understanding Jesus' sufferings on the cross.

In a lounge in the shrine's Retreat House, I meet with Father John Paret, a lean man of sixty with a tanned, bald head. He exudes the kind of wiry energy and wears the kind of 1950s-style sportswear that I associate with boxing coaches. Paret is what the church calls a vice postulate, as Louis Cyr would explain to me, the expert on a particular candidate for sainthood who keeps track of any favours granted through the intercession of prayer. In other words, he's got an eye out for miracles. Kateri has the diligent support of two such men—one in Kahnawake, where she died, and Paret in New York State, near the place where she was born. Before Paret came to Auriesville, he lead a parish in Manhattan, and I tell him that I was just there. On a bright morning I'd walked up Fifth Avenue to look at the statue of Kateri—about three feet tall—fixed to the front door of St. Patrick's Cathedral. It was not easy to get a look at her because a crowd of touring school kids, each clutching a loot bag from Niketown, was clustered in front of the doors. The statue stands, eyes closed, head raised toward the towers of Rockefeller Center across the street. Kateri's hands are turned out at the waist in supplication, and the bronze face is pocked with green, but the artist's work is strong and affecting. This Kateri has a full face with a sizeable nose, expressive lips and a long, flat chin, not the familiar cherubic face of so many icons. There is something sensual about the figure. When you get up close, you're tempted to caress the upturned forehead, stroke the braided hair. I tell Paret that as I moved to leave the church steps a man—middle-aged, carrying a knapsack and a bike helmet—walked up to the statue and did just that, taking Kateri's head in his hand and stroking it, placing his thumb in her palm. Then he went off, smiling.

"What?" he cries, surprised. "No kidding? That's interesting." I tell Paret that on the same day I walked up Fifth Avenue to look at Tekakwitha on the door of St. Patrick's Cathedral I also had visited the streets not far from downtown Brooklyn, where Mohawk steel workers and their families created a neighbourhood in the 1940s and 50s. Once called North Gowanus and now known as Boerum Hill, the area has a strong Islamic presence. The little Cuyler Presbyterian Church still stands on Pacific, where many Mohawks attended services and where the parishioners sponsored a yearly powwow. The two-storey yellow building has been subdivided into private apartments, and when I tried the bell, a voice called from inside.

"Yes?"

"I just wanted to see the church."

"This isn't a church anymore. It's a residence."

"When was it last a church?"

"Twenty-five years ago."

Back on State Street I had sat on a step across from the Devonshire, an impressive red sandstone building that was once full of Mohawk families. People who lived there remember all the doors in the building standing open as neighbours went in and out of one another's apartments. I had even stumbled upon a well-kept wooden building that probably began as a coach house in the mid-1800s and was a Mohawk meeting house in the post-war years. Out front of it, a young black couple had lined up their collection of LPs along with numerous pairs of carefully polished men's shoes, which they were trying to sell. Farther up the street, I had passed the Brooklyn headquarters for Al Sharpton's mayoralty run. Of course, there isn't a Mohawk face in sight.

Paret listens to all this politely and then tells me the history of the Auriesville shrine in detailed terms that make my questions unnecessary.

"We have a place right here," he tells me, "where people actually shed blood for the faith. Joques, Goupil and the others—they came over to teach people about the faith, and here they were put to death."

Of the likelihood of Tekakwitha's becoming a saint, Paret says, "I've given all sorts of reasons why she should be canonized. What we need now is a miracle. The Pope can wave that if he wants to. What he's said is Kateri herself is a miracle. And that's true. She grew up surrounded by people who did not know this faith and really were opposed to it."

I ask Paret whether there is much Mohawk involvement in the shrine's activities. His first expression is one of bafflement and surprise, and then, possibly, embarrassment.

"When I came here in 1990," he tells me, "I saw more Indians than I do now. They come mainly on two occasions. The Sunday nearest the fourteenth of July because that's Kateri's feast day. And they come on the Memorial Day weekend. They used to come from Kahnawake. The last couple years they haven't. They have a powwow at that time now." Paret mentions "a couple or three dozen" Mohawks who still come each year from Syracuse.

When I ask about the relics kept in the shrine's sanctuary, Paret seems a bit uncomfortable.

"I forget now if it's part of her bone or a part of her clothing, but I think it's a part of her bone. Little tiny bit of bone." Paret recovers his characteristic enthusiasm as he describes what he calls "the cures and recent wonderful events" that Catholic believers associate with Kateri.

"A couple years ago a kid took a screwdriver in the eye. The doctors told his parents he could keep the eye for cosmetic purposes, but they would have to get used to the idea that the child would never see with that eye. Not long after, they were visiting someone in North Carolina, and they went to church. The priest was kidding around, and he said to the kid, 'You've got dark glasses on. What are you, a movie star?' So the child explained what happened. And during the service they called the boy up, and they prayed over him to Blessed Kateri. The kid can see now. But the parents won't go and get the medical testimony. And I can write all the letters I want. It's not going to do any good at all until I can get the doctors to testify. And the parents won't agree to let us see the hospital records. I can't understand why they're so reluctant. This is a marvelous blessing the child has received."

To my citified secular imagination, these narratives of private miracles, of devotion to the pieces of the past entombed in Kateri's shrine, sound strangely like tabloid news, fanciful and even a bit sad. But they are clearly alive and real to Paret, who has likely seen most of what there is to see, having worked in Manhattan and Brooklyn.

Once Paret and I have finished our talk, I walk out onto the shrine's sweeping grounds. The New York sky has begun to brighten as the morning's rain clouds burn off. Jackdaws sing from their wet perches. Surrounded by the emptiness of the grounds and the birds' song, I feel at ease. How far this place is from Manhattan and Kateri's upturned face on Fifth Avenue. Even farther from the apartment a friend had lent me in the East Village, where revved up renegades and scrambling artists pursue their idea of a mystery life and search for their own kind of magic and miracles in the cafés and bars.

Stations of the cross near Father Paret's Retreat House

But as I walk farther along the shrine's pathway, I recognize that it includes a model of the stations of the cross, with the twelve tableaux of Jesus' suffering molded in terracotta and set upon brick pedestals. Rather than get off the path, I let myself follow it. The feeling of calm brought on by the weather and birds is replaced by a sense that I am being marched through a bit of theatre with a predictable outcome. Suddenly, the landscape looks surreal and out of whack, and back comes that sinking feeling that I am on the trail of a story that I have no part in.

A wizened old yard worker overturns an Adirondack chair so the previous night's rain will run off. He moves so slowly from one chair to the next that I assume his presence is more decorative than useful. A screwdriver tucked into the rear pocket of his work pants points at the sky when he bends over to grab another chair.

SCREWDRIVERS, as it turned out, would play a more than incidental role in my efforts to get to know Kahnawake and its people. In Toronto I tried, in my low-key way, to connect with a friend whose Cree partner works as a healer in the northern Québec community of Great Whale. I'd met Archie in passing before, but we'd never really talked. Shortly before my trip to New York, I found myself sitting beside him among friends at a backyard barbecue, the perfect chance to ask whether he had any friends in Kahnawake. Archie is a big man—six feet tall, broad across the shoulders, and he carries a fair weight over his belt. He wears his hair long in a pony tail and smiles often beneath the thick lenses of his glasses.

When I tell him I'm planning to follow the trail of Kateri Tekakwitha through New York State and up to Québec, he looks amused and tells me a bit about his friends at Kahnawake. One, named Billy Two Rivers, represented the Mohawk Band Council in discussions with the Québec government during the Oka crisis. There are a couple others who paired up as a wrestling tag team. But Archie doesn't offer to put me in touch with anyone. He lets the subject drop, and we go back to regular dinner conversation.

Once we finish eating, Archie tells a shaggy dog story that he says he uses to warm up crowds at powwows. He tells the story in a voice so quiet that we all have to lean in to hear him. His language changes, taking on a looser, less grammatical shape than it had when he talked casually, and a great deal of what the story leaves unsaid is communicated by the way he holds his hands.

"There's this guy," Archie begins. "Lives out in New Brunswick. He begins to feel there's something wrong with him. The other guys are getting together with the girls, but he finds he can't." Archie cups his hands over his belly, but this gesture clearly suggests a problem lower down. We all listen intently.

"So he goes to the medicine man, and he says, 'I've got this trouble. Here.' And the medicine man says, 'There's someone out on the West Coast who can help you.' So the young man finds his way west and visits this man, who takes a look at him and says, 'I think we can solve your problem. But you have to go up the mountain and stay there for four nights. No eating. No drinking. On the third night you'll get an answer to your problem.'

"The young man goes up the mountain. And by the third night he wishes he was home. He stands"—Archie gets out of his chair and stands, legs spread, arms raised so his fingers touch above his head—"and he calls to the sky. Just as he calls out, he sees a band of light. And coming down through the light is a big screwdriver. The screwdriver fits into his belly and it turns." Archie smiles as he holds his hands before his belly.

"And that screwdriver turns and turns until the screw in the young man's belly falls to the ground. The young man jumps for joy. He jumps and he jumps and he jumps so hard that his ass falls off."

There is a touch of uneasiness in our laughter. A sense of being had. We all bought Archie's act—the healer's gestures, his apparent sharing of tribal wisdom with a nonnative crowd—until the punch line, which suggests that we wouldn't be able to recognize the difference between the wisdom of an elder and one of the older jokes of Groucho Marx. Once I'd thought about it, the way Archie told his story helped me understand his failure to offer his friends up as easy catch for my story-teller's bait. Who was I anyway to Billy Two Rivers of Kahnawake?

ONE WAY TO ARRIVE AT KAHNAWAKE is by Mohawk taxi. Ride the Montréal subway to Angrignon, the last stop, and call the taxi from the station. Fifteen, twenty minutes later a van pulls up outside. Inevitably, the driver picks up someone else on the way through La Salle to the Mercier Bridge. When I ride to the reserve this way, the driver is listening to local talk radio; a doctor is answering questions from callers on everything from the latest flu to how to store molasses (a subject he doesn't claim to know a lot about).

At a mall along the way, we pick up a mother and her young son. The boy holds out a little Swiss Army knife.

"Show him the toothpick, Mom," he calls from the back seat. "Show him the scissors." The boy's fascination with a knife, the boy's mother explains, began with his grandfather's funeral.

"They buried the old man with his knife. And his Copenhagen. They should have put in one of his muskrat traps," she jokes. At the funeral the boy spotted the knife inside the coffin and barely resisted the urge to grab it.

On the bridge we look down at a golf course on the outskirts of the reserve, where natives aren't welcome. But there are two or three others with more genial policies. The taxi meanders through Kahnawake's roads, none of which is named, just as the houses are not numbered. Directions must be given using a healthy dose of *beside that* and *across from there.*

I have no plans, no interviews booked, and no ideas beyond the most obvious: I will visit the church where Tekakwitha's remains are said to be kept. This can be an aimless and risky way to approach an unfamiliar place. The unpredictability can make you shy, so you end up acting like an anonymous tourist, taking pictures and hiding around corners until it's time to get back in the car and go. The first thing I could do is knock on the priest's door at the parish office, but I decide not to. I don't have the heart for it; one superconfident Jesuit telling me stories of kids with miraculously rehabilitated eyes is enough.

I take pictures of the old church with its peeling paint and ragged roof tiles, its attic windows pinned with plastic to keep out the weather. A sign just inside the sanctuary announces an ongoing campaign to collect funds for a new roof. I walk through the museum in the church's rectory. The artifacts stored in glass boxes include a nineteenth-century Iroquois grammar and a bilingual book of Gregorian chants with the Latin originals transliterated into Mohawk. A seventeenth-century oil painting—the oldest that survives—depicts Kateri in a European-style tunic, a black shroud over her head, wearing neat red and yellow lace-up shoes. In the painting's background, an earlier version of the mission sits at the foot of what look like mountains, the New World sky above them in that early morning tangerine hue that reminds even the most cynical of paradise.

In the church kitchen, women are baking sweet-smelling apple pies. And in the gift shop I buy postcards printed in Italy that portray Kateri exuding a healthy Hollywood glow, as well as a mass card bearing a prayer for her canonization:

*A late seventeenth-century
painting of Kateri thought
to be by the Jesuit Claude
Chauchetière*

O GOD, who, among the many marvels of Your Grace in the New World, as *fait fleurir sur les rives de la Mohawk et du Saint-Laurent,* the pure and tender Lily, Kateri Tekakwitha, *daigne nous accorder la grâce que nous te demandons par son intercession . . .*

You can find this prayer on any number of Catholic web sites, in a range of languages, with the urgings of the faithful to pray for Kateri's sainthood.

The women in the church office seem to want me to move along so they can get on with what they are doing. Instead of further investigations into historic French, Jesuit Kahnawake, I walk over to a nondescript, newish building across from the church, where I find the offices of Kahnawake Tourism. There, if anywhere, I think I might hear something of the future of Mohawk Kahnawake.

At the Kahnawake Tourism office I meet Larry McComber, who stands behind the desk and seems a bit surprised at my interest in Tekakwitha—he may take me for some closeted pilgrim—but as I ask questions about the Mohawk community's history, he is quick to talk. McComber's father was one of the many Kahnawake men who chose life on the road as high steel workers, taking jobs on some of Manhattan's biggest modern construction projects, like the Verrazano Bridge and the United Nations General Assembly Building. They worked, as well, on skyscrapers in Buffalo and Detroit.

"My dad took me to New York in 1980," McComber tells me. "He trained me for six weeks. We were on a building on Fifty-Sixth and Fifth, I think it was. I started on the fifteenth floor, going up. That was a shock, but it was supposed to be my career."

In fact, McComber's introduction to high steel work took place just as the American economy and the construction industry went into free fall. Jobs in rivetting gangs began to dry up, and the modest community in Brooklyn made up of ex-Kahnawake Mohawks who worked full time in the States went into its final decline.

After rejecting his father's efforts to bring him into his trade, McComber spent fourteen years as an entrepreneur, before taking the position of spokesman for what might become the main game in town: a tourist and cultural centre planned for Kahnawake, which has received funding from the federal government and would attract visitors from Europe, the United States and Canada for an unusual holiday experience. Visitors can see more than three hundred years of history on the reserve. A house believed to have been lived in by the chief engineer of New France in the early eighteenth century is being painstakingly restored a half block from the tourist office, as an initial improvement in the area's stock of surviving historic buildings.

"We're looking to attract people who will spend somewhere between three and eight days in our hotel and who will spend their money in the community," McComber says. "We have a very special heritage to show them. The native food, dance, art and music. Our social institutions, our material culture and folklore. One big package."

As McComber describes the reserve's economic package, and then explains how far back he can trace his family's presence in Kahnawake, I realize I've entered into a bit of the local dialogue that exists, for the most part, out of earshot of outsiders.

McComber and I meet up later in the afternoon in a board room on the second floor of Kahnawake Tourism's offices. An architectural rendering of the proposed tourist centre stands on a large easel. McComber sets out a file that contains local historical information, his family tree, a recent copy of *Fortune* magazine. Our talk is a typical Canadian mélange: economics, colonialism and identity politics. To Larry McComber, Kateri Tekakwitha is part of the old, dying—if not dead—legacy of French Catholic influence that Kahnawake has been discarding over the past twenty years.

"Tekakwitha plays no significant role in our society today," McComber tells me. According to him, as the role of Christianity fades at Kahnawake, there has been no push from inside the community to take her story back, to retell it in a way that might make it worth something to the contemporary Mohawk imagination.

"People know of her," he says. "They know that in the next few years or so she'll be going through the last stages of becoming a saint. But whether or not these things have an influence on people of my generation, or my children, probably not. I certainly believe that Kateri was a focal point as far as the development of Kahnawake is concerned. I don't have to go back far to see that my dad and my grandmother were devout Catholics. But my father left the church in the early 1960s. There was a tragedy in the family; my brother died, and my dad said, 'If they're going to charge me for the amount of masses that I get, then I'm out.' There was an elitist arrangement where you paid for your prayers, so he left the church. After that he was a Christian unto himself. But he didn't go to church. He pushed me and my brothers and sisters to go, but we could see that it wasn't as important to him as he said it was. I think Christianity has become a thing of the past at Kahnawake. Show me a Sunday when the church is full. Impossible."

I ask how the tourist and cultural centre will make use of the old mission church along with its links to Tekakwitha.

"Look," McComber says, "we're seeing a lot of people from the U.S. and Europe who want to visit the church because of what's happening in their own communities. For them, Kateri's name is symbolic of their beliefs. So if we can take advantage of that and make it part of what we're doing, we will. We'll maintain the church and the fort as best we can. Whether or not they have any positive significance inside the community. I'm not sure what the Jesuits have in mind at this time."

I find it difficult to imagine church leaders like Louis Cyr playing a role in the kind of project McComber is describing, but when you think about it, pilgrimage and tourism aren't all that different. There is a busy worldwide shrine circuit travelled by the faithful, who book junkets that include transportation, accommodation, and food, along with the odd nonreligious side tour to visit the area where a shrine is located. This circuit has turned the most unlikely cites—Kettle River, Minnesota; Knock, Ireland; Fatima, Portugal—into hot spots on travel agents' agendas.

"I know the Jesuits want to be a part of the tourism package," McComber tells me. "Obviously, the church is a sight to be seen. It contains many of the relics from the 1600s. It has historical importance, and we can benefit from that. But it has nothing to do with who we are today."

The quickness with which McComber is able to shuck off aspects of Kahnawake's history like dead skin, dismissing formative stages of European–Mohawk entanglement as meaningless, stands as a stark reminder of how little sympathy many First Nations people feel for traditional Canadian values, customs and history. Still, McComber realizes that the Mohawks of Kahnawake and the various levels of Canadian government remain deeply entangled.

"If we're going to stay here and survive," he adds, "there has to be a lot of cooperation between the provincial government as we push toward self-government. Self-determination, self-government, is going to be a long, arduous process. It's going to be hard to get rid of the old band election system and go back to the original clans and clan mothers. Plus, we're at the mercy of the government for dollars. We have so little economic development. But I don't think we'll see the day again when either the province or the country will be able to put their foot inside our door, expropriate land or determine who's who in our community. Those days are over. The only thing we want from them is the dollars that are due to us. We want to build our economy. We are a nation. And we have a face that we show. We are divided along many lines, but we have to show solidarity. If someone dropped the question of whether we wanted to go to war again as happened in 1990, we'd have to all say yes."

WAR IN CANADA? Now there's something most Canadians would find hard to imagine. But in effect, there was a kind of war fought between Mohawks and the Canadian military in 1990 as the dispute over a golf course development on tribal land at Oka led to blockades at Kahnawake and Kanehsatake (the reserve beside the contested tribal lands). One of the disruptive effects of these struggles for Montréalers was the Mohawk blockade of the Mercier Bridge, the main crossing between the city and the south shore suburbs and towns. The stand-offs became even more complicated as a radical warrior leadership confronted elected band leaders. Within native ranks there was serious and at times violent disagreement over the role of casinos and the cigarette trade on reserve land. But the disturbances also led to an historic gathering of 150 chiefs at Kahnawake and an uncommonly unified call for the resolution of land claims.

Although the Oka stand-off received a disproportionate amount of attention in the press, it may be the response among Mohawks of Kahnawake and nearby reserves that provides the most telling lesson Canadians can take from the events of 1990. The blockades at Kahnawake and Kanehsatake not only challenged abusive expropriation of tribal land, but brought into question the national borders of Canada and the United States. Lurking behind such inflammatory issues as cigarette smuggling, tax-exempt casinos and moves by promoters to mount "extreme fighting" competitions on Mohawk land are difficult questions of economic and cultural self-determination. Although the militarism of the Mohawk Warriors and the possibility of a response by the Canadian military distracted most Canadians from these longstanding issues, calmer times present an opportunity to consider them as guiding concerns motivating the Mohawk response to the Oka town council's plans to expand a golf course onto tribal land.

With hindsight, the events surrounding the blockades look like a public relations disaster for Canadian natives. The summer of 1990 offered unparalleled attention from media, government and social groups, which was in part squandered as the public remained transfixed by images of a gun-toting Warrior named Lasagna. Louis Cyr told me the stand-off left native–Québec relations worse than they'd ever been. Businesses in Chateauguay, near Kahnawake, which relied on native clientele, had lost out. "Relations have been thwarted for at least a generation or two," Cyr said.

Some time after speaking with Larry McComber about the tourist centre plans for Kahnawake, I meet Kenneth Deer, who owns and edits *The Eastern Door,* a smart local newspaper serving the Kahnawake community. Deer sits down at a desk in the newspaper's back office and asks, "How can I help you?"

He tells me that the tourist centre and cultural complex plans have failed. By announcing the project before they had a business plan, the town council had put the cart before the horse. They'd been given $500,000 by the federal government, and Deer thinks they might have spent as much as $700,000 before the big plans dried up.

"If they make Kateri Tekakwitha a saint," Deer says, "I don't know how we'll handle the influx." His eyes squint shut as he smiles. The idea of a pilgrim rush on Kahnawake's main road seems to amuse him.

Overall, things in Kahnawake have been relatively calm over the last few years. There's a new hospital building and a powwow advertised as a tourist event each summer. But if you drive into Kahnawake on a whim, looking for a gas station or a sandwich, you might not realize you're in a reserve town. As drivers pass under the Mercier Bridge, the small group working on the span are too high up to be recognized as Mohawks. At the corner store a poster might advertise a George Jones concert sponsored by the reserve radio station later in the summer. And the NOs spray-painted on the back of stop signs (someone's way of opposing a casino proposal) look like nothing more than a teenage prank. But in how many other places in Canada would the trim, businesslike character manning the desk at the local tourist office talk about the possibility of going to war with the provincial and federal governments?

GERALD T. ALFRED, a Kahnawake-born Mohawk who teaches in the Political Science Department at the University of Victoria, views the radicalization of reserve politics during the Oka crisis in a positive light, but not because he believes there is any prospect of war.

"I think 1990 was good for us," Alfred tells me over the phone from his Victoria home. "It was an episode in our relearning process because it eliminated the option of a militant, confrontational strategy. What you saw with the leaders of those stand-offs was people dressing as Mohawks—and as leaders—but not acting as though they were either. They announced their interest in reviving the Longhouse structure without relying on true Longhouse values. So after 1990 we found that militarism did not present viable principles to build on. For all of us it was an opportunity to be more philosophical, more adaptive, to reach a deeper understanding of who we are."

Like McComber, Gerald Alfred's roots in Kahnawake go back many generations. They include intermarriage between Mohawks and whites; and like McComber, Alfred comes from what he calls a mainstream family. One grandmother, who was white, started the successful Rabaska Restaurant on land where the family had previously run a grocery store. Before going into business, Alfred's family on his mother's side were successful corn farmers who also managed their own orchards. And like McComber's father, Alfred's made his living—and continued to at age fifty-six—as an iron worker. Gerald Alfred's most striking break with his family background is the energy with which he committed himself to, and excelled in, his pursuit of a university career. After completing studies at Concordia and Cornell, he found he was one of only three or four native political scientists in North America, and he has been the chair of the Native American Studies Association of America. Though he lives on the West Coast, Alfred maintains his ties to Kahnawake. He has been a senior advisor to Chief Joe Norton's Band Council, and in 1995 he published *Heeding the Voices of Our Ancestors: Kahnawake Mohawk Politics and the Rise of Native Nationalism*, which brings together his professional and personal concerns.

Alfred likens the history of the Kahnawake area to the open cities that flourished in Europe early in the century, where no neighbouring power held total sway, and changing trade alliances ensured a free-wheeling, often transient population.

"Our people migrated north a couple thousand years ago from what we would now call Ohio," he explains. In precolonial times the bulk of Mohawk land lay near the Mohawk River Valley, and when I mention that I'd been to Auriesville, where Father Paret's shrine stands, he tells me, "As far as we're concerned that land is still ours. The French signed treaties with three people who were exiles. They had no right to sign away our land. As a Mohawk it's sickening to go there. It just makes you sad. The land across from Montréal was on the northern margin of Mohawk territory. The whole Montréal area was an area where our people traded and moved around. It's always been the position of the Jesuits and the French that they led the Mohawks to the Kahnawake area. But the Mohawks were taking advantage of a situation—especially for trade. The only consistency on the white side in this area is the use of Kahnawake as a centre of illicit trade—first in furs—to circumvent official French and British trade circuits. More recently, with cigarettes, we were useful for the same reason."

If the band's proposal for an elaborate tourist centre had taken off, a more gentle sort of trade might well have redefined the relationship between Mohawks and the rest of Canada. Religion, the other consistent meeting ground between these two solitudes, is no longer a relevant point of cultural interaction, according to Gerald Alfred.

"The influence of Christianity at Kahnawake is almost nil," Alfred tells me. "There's a lot of nominal Christians who still get their kids baptized and get married in the church. There's a need for the ceremonial aspect of Catholicism. It means something to people who can count nine generations of their family in the parish records who were baptized at that church. But at the same time, if you go to midnight mass, people are rolling their eyes. There's been such a strong effort to recover our traditional ways; a consciousness of our history makes it impossible to believe. It's not just the younger people who've turned against it. Former altar boys and former wannabe priests are also leading us away. One of the events of 1990 that didn't get talked about much will give you an idea of where we've come to. Two or three of the Longhouse women went to the church and demanded the bones of Kateri Tekakwitha back. They believed she was being appropriated and used as a Mohawk woman. A lot of the Mohawks feel she's a captive still, that her spirit is captive. The women wanted to take her and give her a proper burial, with a Longhouse ceremony and a death feast. The kind of mourning that would pacify her spirit."

When I ask Alfred how the parish priest responded to these demands, he says he doesn't know. But it's the act of demanding Tekakwitha's remains and not the outcome (which was a failure) that is most telling. Clearly, the three-hundred-year-old story of the world's most famous Mohawk has lost some of its authority and is viewed by Mohawk traditionalists as little more than a cynically constructed fairy tale.

Alfred admits that there is no oral tribal record—no reliable historical consciousness—of Kateri, but the demand of the Longhouse women suggests that, as a paradigmatic captive, Tekakwitha has taken on meaning that is relevant in contemporary Kahnawake, at least to its women. Alfred even suggests that her canonization might have the effect of affirming traditional Mohawk identity.

"It's true that a lot of natives will be happy. There's pride in the fact that she's a Mohawk and she's world renowned. It'll be a chance to evaluate our relationship to Catholicism. I think it would be a good time to hold a conference. Make it a critical event. But there will be no outpouring of Catholic ceremonialism. Ten years ago. Fifteen years ago, maybe. Now it's just such a bankrupt concept. Catholicism is seen as a viable religion—just not ours."

As I visit Kahnawake and talk to people about it, I often feel that my earnest questions are viewed with a kind of sympathetic pity. What could I expect to learn as an outsider? And when I explain that Tekakwitha is my focus, I must seem desperately out of it, either an old-fashioned believer or a researcher with some kind of fetishistic relationship with the dusty leather-bound volumes in Jesuit archives.

"It's other people who are obsessed with her, not us," Alfred said of Tekakwitha.

I get the same bemused, slightly baffled response from Margo Kane, whom I interview over coffee on Vancouver's Denman Street. The afternoon we meet is rainy and warm, and as with most coffee bars in the city, the place we've chosen is full of boisterous escapees from the damp. Kane played the role of Tekakwitha in a 1987 production *The Lily of the Mohawks,* which was written by British playwright Patricia Rodriquez and staged at Montréal's prestigious Saidye Bronfman Theatre. Kane is an Edmonton-born Cree—looking less Cree as she ages, she tells me with a laugh. She weathered her share of difficult seasons in the 1970s, when roles for nonwhite actors in Canada were difficult to find. An early disappointment came when Edmonton's Citadel Theatre staged George Ryga's *The Ecstasy of Rita Joe,* a celebrated play about the clash between reserve and city life. The director chose Kane to understudy the white Texas actress who played the lead role of a native woman from British Columbia.

"I spent ten years," Kane says, "being the only brown face that played every role that was an ethnic role in the Canadian theatre because I happened to look a little different."

In the early 1980s Kane did get a chance to tour as Ryga's Rita Joe, and I ask her whether Ryga's play or the Tekakwitha role meant more to her.

"Rita Joe was more important to me. It spoke to me," she explains. "All our people, no matter what religion, end up in town. Many end up on the skids, in low income places, struggling and falling between the cracks. Whereas Tekakwitha's experience was—well, I was uncomfortable with it. It didn't possess me as Rita Joe did. I see Rita Joes all the time, or I did. Rita Joe connected me with my community. With the Tekakwitha play, the rest of the cast but for one was nonnative. And I would continue to deal with that sort of situation for a number of years till I just threw up my hands."

Like most of the native people I talk with, Kane has not read Leonard Cohen's celebrated novel *Beautiful Losers*, which uses Tekakwitha as a focal point around which the author creates a surreal portrait of the political, sexual and social upheavals of 1960s Montréal. In Cohen's fictional city there is a plastic reproduction of Kateri on the dashboard of every Montréal taxi. She becomes for him a Mohawk Marilyn Monroe: mythic and magically alluring in her tragic death.

When Kane spent her first winter in Montréal to rehearse and play Kateri, she found no such enthusiasm for the Jesuit's creation.

"My sense was that she has little or no relevance in Western pop culture. Especially in Montréal. That was my feeling then and that is my feeling now. Leonard Cohen may be the only person who's written her name in all of Montréal since the Jesuits wrote back to France about her."

Kane too is clearly baffled by the interest among nonnatives in certain native figures. Thinking back to her work on the play, she realizes she never knew what it was about Tekakwitha that entranced the play's producer and its author.

"I was unsure about the writer," she admits. "I was unsure about everybody's motivation."

And "everybody" must include me, with my hope of uncovering, through Tekakwitha's story, a crossing place between my own experiences as a first-generation Canadian and those of contemporary Mohawks. I assume that we share, even with our vastly different experience, a mistrust of the Canadian status quo and its willingness to present the country as a place of open borders, as a warm and tasty multicultural stew, though I know that Mohawk mistrust is of a deeper and far more intransigent nature.

SOMEHOW, my visit to Kahnawake and Auriesville, and my talk with Louis Cyr, make my feeling of disconnection with native Canada even greater. Louis Cyr and I talk a long time, as the day grows cold and the winter light shuts down. Cyr explains that what is entombed in his church's sanctuary is most properly called the remains of Tekakwitha. "Relics," he tells me, "are pieces you extract from those and enshrine in a container for the veneration of the faithful."

As late as the 1970s, relics associated with Tekakwitha were stored in a box, tied with ribbons, that could be brought out for visitors. The box was the sort of thing that somebody could walk away with, and one day somebody almost did, so a more secure arrangement was devised, and Tekakwitha's relics were entombed in marble.

Later, I wonder about this near-heist. Was the would-be thief native? Maybe he had dreamed of releasing the bit of bone from its box just to see if there was anything to the idea that a captive spirit required attention and a proper burial. Maybe he was interested in taking home a little bit of Indian Canada, the vanished world of the Mohawks before the French, the British and the Americans. Maybe he was interested in making her over yet again in his own image, like Andy Warhol did in his silkscreen portraits of the Sioux chief Sitting Bull. In these, Sitting Bull, after his capture, is given a sharp pop-art glow. His jersey is the colour of a Dakota pumpkin, his face the rich indigo of expensive jeans, the arrow upright on his head a psychedelic blue-black. Sitting Bull, the great legend of courage on the Great Plains, is transformed into pop currency, into lucre in the pocket of a gallery owner.

So it goes with Kateri Tekakwitha in her travels through the minds of Jesuits, Mohawks, believers and the business planners of band councils—successive generations each taking up their brushes to retouch history in their own image.

Landscape's Narrative

DOING THE MALCOLM LOWRY WALK

I N A STUNNING late nineteenth-century photograph of the shoreline town site called Granville, later renamed Vancouver, swirls of wood smoke rise above the cedars and the few structures in view. This was no calamitous fire, but the founding of a city. To begin settlement, the surrounding forest had to be cleared and burned. This photo shouldn't give one the impression, however, that the forest was an uninhabited paradise, a jungle of cedar and fir wrapped in primeval sunlight and rains. Think of the swirl of smoke rising into the Pacific blue as a fearsome housecleaning—a send-off of earlier versions of coastal life the settlers had decided to replace with what they called home.

Things change fast on the West Coast. At least they have in the past century. More times than we can count, one village has been thrown out in favour of another town, which is in turn replaced by a newer city. Our understanding of these changes is hampered by the lack of popular chronicles devoted to these events. The photo of the burning of Granville is a weird apparition from the past, its maker as dead as the wood he watched burn. Imagine what this viewer could tell us of the disappearing habitat he photographed as a new one emerged.

A similar missed opportunity to chronicle the remaking of Vancouver's North Shore—the land across Burrard Inlet from Stanley Park—can be found in the voluminous writings of novelist Malcolm Lowry. A transplanted Englishman who lived for fourteen years in a squatter's shack on the North Shore's Dollarton Flats, Lowry was perfectly positioned to capture the final disappearance of Squamish coastal life as it was replaced by its antithesis: the burgeoning suburban streets of modern post-war residential developments. On a government foreshore beach, in a community of shacks established by millwrights working at the nearby Dollar Mill, Lowry set up house in one of the temporary communities that were constantly appearing on the outskirts of recent development, only to be removed when a new version of the area under renovation was completed.

Squatting is an old and established tradition in British Columbia. During the Depression it was often the saving grace of men without work, and after the Second World War, when housing shortages brought on by a boom in Vancouver left many workmen unable to afford a home, makeshift communities—called slums in the local newspapers—sprung up in coastal pockets within travelling distance of mill and shipbuilding sites.

The longest-lived of these was the little squatter village of Dollarton on the North Shore of the Burrard Inlet, not far from Deep Cove. In its earliest incarnation, the village was populated by shack dwellers who worked at John Dollar's big mill or at nearby Mckenzie Barge and Derrick. At its height, the village had ninety shacks scattered along the Dollarton flats. The squats at Dollarton met their demise in the winter of 1971, after more than fifteen years of eviction notices and court orders. Most of the squatters, from raffia-making hippies to the families of university professors, had already left or put the torch to their wooden homes by the time the city's bulldozers arrived.

The first and arguably least heroic squatters in British Columbia were the early pioneers who squatted on coastal Salish and Squamish land when they arrived from the Prairies or the northern States in search of gold or pelts or a cheap way to harvest timber. These men set up a tent, got the fire lit and hung a pot out for some of the good strong coffee they would need to take their minds off the work that lay ahead. The Squamish, whose population was spread over both shores of the Burrard Inlet and up the coast of the mainland, traded with these settlers; sometimes native women married them; and gradually, as the town sites of these squatter–pioneers thrived, they began to displace Squamish village sites, which the settlers were quick to identify as squatter camps on crown land.

It's hard today to imagine a Squamish village where the foot of the Burrard Street Bridge stands. Cities aren't allowed to work this way, especially in boom time, when every bit of spare land, marsh and waterside looks ripe for change and profit. Add to this the fact that when Canadian municipalities feel flush, an ethic of tidiness reigns supreme. Little squat communities of fishermen, bohemians or natives displaced by pioneering development are easily characterized as a bad example, as breeding grounds of crime, disease and worse.

LOWRY, who left Canada for England before the end of Dollarton's squatter community, wrote the bulk of his life's work on the beach. But he was largely uninterested in these local developments for the purposes of his fiction. His imagination shambled off to Mexico and F. Scott Fitzgerald's Hollywood, while the story of his daily life on the shores of the Burrard Inlet was commented on mainly in letters to friends.

Death and taxes were exactly what the North Shore District Council believed Malcolm Lowry deserved as it delivered its eviction notices to him and his fellow squatters like little letter bombs from an angry god. The north shore of the inlet across from Stanley Park was being hurriedly subdivided in the early 1950s, and squatters were not a particularly strong selling point when a salesman brought a prosperous young family—with the statistically correct number of kids, cars and insurance packages—to view a lot cut out of the forest in the area Lowry dubbed Dark Roslyn. Lowry was caught between his desire to live like a woodsman philosopher at the edge of modern life and the city's urge to push itself farther up the mountainside, to take back the land covered in second growth after men like John Dollar had made a fortune feeding the first growth into his mill.

In a lifetime of often fretful but more or less constant writing,

Malcolm Lowry began and finished (by finished I mean published) only two books of fiction: *Ultramarine,* a young man's novel of the sea, and *Under the Volcano.* The latter, substantially rewritten at least three times and rejected by publishers in a variety of forms, arrived at its final shape while Lowry and his wife, Margerie Bonner, lived in a shack on the foreshore of a Canadian government harbour across from a city just beginning what would be one of a number of staggering post-war booms.

Ironically, this particular place where Lowry finally finished his book always represented for him new beginnings. In a 1945 letter he described his shack and its neighbours along the Dollarton Flats as the "last example" of "pioneer activity" on the Vancouver waterfront. And this sense of Dollarton being a place to begin anew in an unspoiled world returns again and again in Lowry's shorter fiction—much of it unfinished at his death. "The Forest Path to the Spring," an autobiographical story Lowry worked on until late in his life, includes a kind of psalm to squatter life at Dollarton.

Upon first arriving on the beach, Lowry's narrator finds summering city folk baking clams, and encounters the remnants of an oil slick loosed from a tanker, but he and his wife recognize the promise of "absolute emptiness and solitude" on this tide flat "covered with huge barnacled rocks . . . and exoskeletons of crabs." Lowry recognized something primordial and benignly inhuman about this place of slime and ancient stones. And at first glance, for the narrator in "The Forest Path to the Spring," the flats are a peopleless landscape. For the greater part of the year, Lowry noted, he and his wife were often alone at Dollarton. He described his beach house and its surroundings as though they existed outside modern history or at least as part of a prehistory forgotten by modern men and women. The wooden piles that support his shack looked to him

> like a strange huge cage where some amphibious animal might
> have lived . . . when often at low tide, resetting a cross-brace,
> amidst the seaweed smells, I felt as if I were down in the first

slime . . . I delighted in the simplicity of the stresses of the foundations I was looking at . . . [which] were of course above ground, as in the most primitive of all houses.

But, of course, such portraits of Dollarton as a kind of Pacific Eden, as a peopleless garden where an author could gain perspective on himself and his work, are among Lowry's finest fictions. He was a latecomer to these parts and no pioneer at all.

In 1940, when Lowry arrived at Dollarton, there were two important established communities in the area, one of which interested him greatly and entered the version of the landscape he would tell in his fiction; the other remained more or less out of his view and invisible to his readers. Lowry came to know and love the little community of deep-sea fishermen who had built many of the shacks that lined the Dollarton Flats. A number of these men were transplanted Brits like Lowry, and his respect for them seems to have been partly founded on a sentimental attachment to his roots and his own seafaring youth. In "The Forest Path to the Spring," Lowry depicts this fishing community as a "sort of town, by the sawmill round the northward point," where "two hamlets" could be found—one made up of shacks with names and another of houses without names. The owners of houses with names like Hangover and Wywurk were city people who came to their beach shacks "for the weekend in summer, or for a summer holiday of a week or two." Lowry viewed such people as interlopers who passed time on the beach until they could afford to buy a ritzier summer cottage and then look down on the squatters at Dollarton.

The owners of the unnamed houses were fishermen who, Lowry says, were accorded some kind of foreshore rights because of their trade. Lowry describes their departure in early summer as if they are journeymen out of an unsung Canadian epic: "these fishermen went away, sometimes singly, sometimes in pairs, sometimes three or four boats joined together . . . newly painted fishing boats with their tall gear would be seen going round the point." Around Labour Day, just as the weekenders went back to the city, these men would reappear to reconstitute what Lowry describes as a kind of sacred tribe:

> The unmarried fisherman often lent their shacks to their friends in the summer, but they were sacrosanct when they returned . . . the attitude of the solitary fisherman toward his shack, and his boat was not dissimilar. In effect his love for the one was like his love for the other . . . their little cabins were shrines of their own integrity and independence, something that this type of human being, who seems almost to have disappeared, realizes can only be preserved without the evil of gossip. And actually each man's life was in essence a mystery. . . .

The shacks of these men are like shrines, monkish retreats, as integral to their surroundings in Lowry's view as a Shinto temple is to the Japanese landscape. The fishermen of Dollarton are honourable for being removed from all modern coastal developments; it is their outsider status that marks them as endangered apostles of a truer way of life. Lowry describes their shacks as "the only human dwellings visible on this side of the water that had any air of belonging . . . some dark and tumbledown, others freshly and prettily painted . . . all standing, even the most somber, with their fluted tin chimneys smoking here and there like toy tramp steamers, as though in defiance of the town, before eternity."

Lowry is right about the shacks' look of humble integrity and independence; with windowpanes set carefully into their wood plank walls and a tin stove-pipe smoking under the cover of trees, nothing appeared dashed together or haphazard about these squats. In old photographs the shacks look snug and inviting, some with a peaked roof or a balcony overlooking the water, others with elaborate piers built out from the shoreline so that the tide could come sweeping in around the piers' foundation posts and stop just short of the elevation at which the deck or the door line of the shack was set. At high tide the shacks and piers appeared to be

The Dollarton shacks where Lowry lived, with their elaborate homemade piers

floating on the water, as seabirds, otters and seals came looking to see what creature it was that squatted on stilts sunk into the tide's depths.

When Lowry describes his love of the local fishermen, he no longer talks of Dollarton as if it were a primitive, peopleless site, but instead, as though it were hallowed ground where hard-working monks perform their honest devotions. The moon, clouds and mountain behind the cedars take on a silhouette reminiscent of the great European cathedrals. In *Under the Volcano* the characters imagine a Canadian idyll, where inhabitants turn to the east like devotees in a vast prayer house, and silence reigns under the "white white distant alabaster thunderclouds beyond the mountains, the thunderless gold lightning in the blue evening, unearthly." In contrast with the novel's hellish Mexican landscape, the inlets of British Columbia are adorned like the inner sanctum of some holy of holies, washed in imperial gold and purple, the sky a vaulted ceiling covered in a fresco of sculpted clouds worthy of Michelangelo. For Lowry, the opposites of his forest sanctuary are the fleshpots and ash heaps of Vancouver, a short boat ride across the inlet.

On a beautiful August day I borrow a car and drive to meet Harvey Burt, who lives at Deep Cove, a short drive from the flats where Lowry and his wife lived in a sequence of three shacks: one rented, one bought and burned to the ground, the third built with wood pulled in by the tide.

Burt was a constant friend and neighbour to the Lowrys. With his wife, Dorothy, Burt took care of the Lowrys' third shack when they left Canada for Europe. Some of the last and easily the saddest of Lowry's letters were addressed to Burt, as the writer, trying desperately to work in faraway Ripe, England, expressed heartbreak about the news that the pier he'd built had been swept away in a storm.

I want to talk with Burt, not so much about Lowry himself, as about what it was like to live in the kind of squatter's community that flourished on Vancouver beachfronts in the decades after the war. But I head to our meeting with some trepidation. In my correspondence with him, Burt was straightforward though a touch testy as he wrote of the investment of time and knowledge he and his wife had already offered authors hunting up information on Lowry. And friends, he wrote to me, had persuaded him that he "owes it to posterity" to record his experience of life on the beach. Still, in a postscript at the bottom of his letter, Burt added, "I am, however, quite willing to escort you along the beach when you come this way."

I lived in Vancouver for seven years in the 1980s, the last good years, a sentimentalist might say, before Expo '86 put the stake in the heart of an older Vancouver and ushered in a faster, shinier, slightly meaner version. During the summer of 1986, a lot of local restaurants and businesses closed because most of the tourist money coming to town was spent on the Expo site. Newspapers reported a sequence of high-profile deaths of old-timers who were pulled from flophouses that were being renovated as hotel suites for tourists. I had managed to go most of the summer without entering the fair until a friend visiting from Calgary wanted to see it, and I had to hide my distaste and escort him to see all the pointless exhibits that had been set up on the shore of False Creek.

During my years in Vancouver, the closest I got to North Vancouver and Dollarton on anything like a regular basis was when I drove over the Lion's Gate Bridge to turn, not east toward the flats, but west toward Horseshoe Bay, where the ferry departs for Vancouver Island. Once, on a night so stormy the Lions Gate Bridge seemed to shiver in the wind's gusts, my girlfriend and I did go east in the direction of Dollarton, and then to the top of Lonsdale Avenue to visit a friend who wanted to show us the house she'd grown up in. We discovered later in the week from the police, and from the report of an attendant who manned a guardhouse on the bridge, that my girlfriend's brother had, at roughly the hour we were passing over the bridge, got up on the barriers of its pedestrian walkway and jumped, disappearing forever into Lowry's beloved inlet.

So the Lion's Gate, with its magnificent miles-long view of both the eastern and western waters, of dappled light on the inlet's surface and of the big-nosed merchant ships lined up to enter the port, has a haunted quality for me. Its monumental presence is full of a young man's absence. If you look east from the bridge's height, past the mouth of the Seymour River and along the irregular north shore of the inlet, dotted with ship landings, mounds of sulphur and lumber waiting to be loaded, you can see the triangle of land jutting into the water near Deep Cove called Roche Point.

I leave myself enough time to get lost on my way to Harvey Burt's house, the map on the seat beside me. Burt and I have made plans to walk in Cates Park, a typically handsome park cut into what was once the wooded shore of Roche Point. At the southeast end of the park—with a view across the inlet of the tip of Burnaby Mountain, the Canadian Pacific Railway tracks and an oil refinery—is the beach where Lowry and Burt had their shacks.

Not wanting to be late for my meeting with this man who's seen a few too many scribblers with a tape recorder and a long list of questions, I arrive in Harvey Burt's neighbourhood early enough to stop at Starbucks for one of the elaborately named beverages formerly known as a cup of coffee. Their North Shore location is in a newish mall nestled at the bottom of the Mount Seymour forest along the Dollarton Highway.

A Squamish graveyard, with a view of Burnaby in the distance, where another squatter colony thrived between the railway and the shoreline

I can't bring myself to ask for any of the frillier drinks, which seem to take their names from Italian film stars, so I order a Café Americano, irritating the woman who serves me by asking for a medium, rather than the tall that is keeping stockholders happy, happy, happy. I sit at a counter by the window and look over the headlines in the August 28 *North Shore News*. Like some ghost that won't stay buried, the Dollarton waterfront continues to be the source of debates. For the third time in eight years, residents will examine the merits of development on the waterfront. Promising public access to the water and parks—the same baubles that local government offered as replacements for the squatter shacks in the 1950s and '60s—United Properties Ltd. has proposed a "multi-storey development" on a six-acre site, which was once the operation site of Mckenzie Barge and Marineways. Many of the men who worked at Mckenzie Barge in the 1940s and '50s found affordable (as good as free) living arrangements in shacks near Lowry's and Burt's.

The disappearance of Mckenzie Barge came up in a phone conversation I'd had not long before with Bill Gaston, a novelist and short story writer who grew up at Deep Cove but was teaching and writing in New Brunswick. When I asked Gaston what had changed about Dollarton since the late 1960s, when he was a teenager, he mentioned the plan to put condos on the old Mckenzie Barge site. He mentioned as well the disappearance of Burrardview grade school on Dollarton Highway, where, from the classroom window, he'd watched deer and bear trundle by. In Gaston's day the forest at the edge of Cates Park had not yet been dolled up, and the path through it had not been renamed the Malcolm Lowry Walk.

"It was mud," Gaston said of the path through the forest that is now named for Lowry. "There was no gravel. No historic markers."

One thing that had remained unchanged from shortly after the war until the late 1960s was the little community of squatter shacks down by the tide's edge.

"But there wasn't much connection between us locals and the shack guys," Gaston told me. "Occasionally, we'd meet somebody. There might have been some kind of midnight fire connection. But we saw them as outsiders in a way. They were older—hippies. A lot of the guys there were a bit on the way out." Gaston remembers Al Neil—the eclectic musician–writer–artist—living on the beach around 1970. Gaston's brother once picked Neil up as he thumbed for a ride along the highway and asked his passenger how he was doing. Neil growled and took a bite out of the car's foam dashboard. So the squatter life—once a worker's necessity, then a writer's imagined paradise of solitude—had been taken up by the bohemian musicians and social rebels of Vancouver's summer of love. A new band of outsiders was trying to find a space—just a few hundred yards wide by a mile or two long—where they might live out their dreams.

"It was a wild time," Gaston said of the area in the 1960s and early '70s. "And you have to remember," he added, "the Cove and Dollarton—they're on a geographical edge. You can't go any farther in one direction. That made it a frontier, which brought out a certain kind of cool in peo-

ple—a Wild West attitude. It was very much cowboy drinking and dev-
ilish stunts, psychic stunts, craziness."

I make my way to the Burts' house along winding roads named for
British land surveyors, enterprising mill owners, birds and sea shells.
There is a Roslyn Boulevard—Lowry's boulevard of broken dreams—
and a patently incongruous Lowry Lane. The Burts' house is one of the
older bungalows built on the outskirts of Deep Cove, which looks
directly at the calm waters a short way along the shoreline from
Dollarton Beach. The house has the eclectic look of many post-war
Vancouver homes: the figure of a bird is etched on the garage door with
feathers pinned to the wood for a tail. The entranceway is small and
might be a homemade job, using what looks like unfinished boards
rounded up at a nearby lumberyard. Through the big living room window we look across the water at an expensive-looking house of wood
and rock that someone has built on a tiny private island. Beyond it is the
south shore of the inlet where the Barnet Highway and the rail line
snake off to the west.

Harvey Burt, getting on but looking outdoorsy in shorts and a short-
sleeved shirt, stands and points across the water. "There were shacks
along that south shore too," he tells me. He points at a bare spot on the
far bank, where pilings mark the old site of the Barnet Mill. "From there,
in to the Second Narrows Bridge, there were shacks all along there. I
knew some people who lived down where the Chevron refinery is. There's
a little bay in there. There was a real community of people with a number of floats, and one guy had a store."

The Burts represent a very particular slice of shore life from Lowry's
day. Unlike Lowry, the affordability of squatter life was not what landed
them at Dollarton. Burt taught high school and his wife, Dorothy, was
accustomed to the comfortable life her father, a doctor, offered his children. The Burts travelled often in years when Canadians did not take
international travel for granted as they do now, and they always had a permanent home they could return to when the novelty of their shack wore
off or the weather turned.

I ask Burt what became of this makeshift shore town on what is now parkland, docks and rail right-of-way across the inlet.

"All those shacks were burned in the summer of 1960," he says. "I can remember thinking of Troy. Both the CPR and the Federal Harbours Board objected to people crossing over the tracks."

This decree of the big powers in the neighbourhood reminds me of the little rules we impose on children—neatly combed hair, properly tied shoes, sitting up straight at the table—regulations that ensure orderliness at the expense of the spiritedness and joy that come with certain harmless disorderly ways.

Nobody thinks nowadays about the little shacks on the inlet's south shore because no famous writer was evicted there, after sweating blood over draft after draft of novel, short story and screenplay. It may be fair to say that the squatter life at Dollarton owes its fame not to Malcolm Lowry, but to Lowry's wife, Margerie Bonner, who noticed a newspaper ad one July afternoon for a cottage for rent in the hamlet of Dollarton: "Two rooms. Outhouse up the hill. Rent $15 per month."

Contrary to his stand-offish letter, Burt offers me a fine lunch. He, his wife, and I eat quiche and salad and talk about the usual Canadian subjects: the difference between living in Toronto and Vancouver, a CBC show playing on the radio that sits on the window sill. After lunch Burt and I drive to the edge of Cates Park, each in our own car so he can leave me when we're through. We stop near a tennis court and get out, setting off to the lazy rhythm of a ball being knocked back and forth behind the trees.

CATES PARK was dedicated in 1950 to the memory of Captain Charles H. Cates, a Canadian pioneer in the truest sense. Cates was born in 1859 in Maine and grew up in the Maritimes, working the schooners that carried coal from Nova Scotia to St. John, New Brunswick. He went west in his twenties, working on the railroad (he was at Craigalachie when Lord Strathcona drove the last spike) and on a work crew that surveyed the prairie near Winnipeg. When he arrived on the coast in 1886, Vancouver was a newly incorporated town site, having just abandoned the name of

Granville chosen by its original settlers. His first business involved chartering vessels that hauled lumber he bought for next to nothing in town. He took the wood north to supply the needs of Skagway in the Yukon, where the gold rush was in full swing. The Cates family business would eventually become the biggest marine hauling concern on the North Shore.

There can be no arguing that Cates left his mark on the lower mainland. His biography is quintessentially Canadian: the American family coming north, the young man going west to make his mark on the frontier. But the idea for a park nestled among the trees above the Dollarton flats owed as much to the memory of Cates as to a rising dislike for the community of shacks down on the beach. As early as 1947 Lowry had been described in a Vancouver newspaper as the "King of the beach squatters." Though he "could write a cheque for thousands," the article claimed, Lowry lived rent and tax free on public land. In 1950 the first in a long sequence of eviction notices went out, telling the squatters they would have to move or be moved.

As Burt and I walk west into the forested side of the park, he points behind us to where John Dollar had his mill.

"It was one block that way," Burt tells me, waving beyond the trees at an established neighbourhood street. "And all of this was Dollar property. It was a company village, just to the east there. They had a school, a grocery, a church. The workers lived in shacks," he adds with a smile. "They were squatters too." Always these necessary labourers—the men who do a job but don't quite fit into the city their work helps build, and, in the long run, are hustled off as quietly as possible.

As we follow the wooded path, the flats a few hundred yards down the hill on our left, Burt's walking stick makes a solid metallic sound as it traces his steps. It is one of those mellow, fragrant Vancouver afternoons, so perfect it can break your heart. In my university days I took afternoons like this more or less for granted, reading my course books on a bench in front of Main Library, a coffee at hand, the cedar bench giving off its own fragrance as the sun heated and dried the last rains out of it.

The Malcolm Lowry Walk, which is located on parkland near where North Vancouver evicted its squatters

"Now this has all grown up since Lowry lived here," Burt says of the surrounding forest. "In those days it was all covered with blackberries. And there was never any grass here. No pine trees. Those have all been planted. The whole thing's been tidied up in a typical landscape artist's fashion."

Burt wants to show me the paths the Lowrys used to take to the bus, to the store and to fetch water. He even points out the route that led to the shithouse, as he quite accurately calls the meager amenities of squatter living. I try to get Burt's opinion on the more substantial path that runs along the shore, which the city named for Lowry, reclaiming as its own the man it had once so energetically tried to run off its land. But Burt has little interest in the gussied up stretch of forest where benches have been placed with meditative views of the water. I ask if he thinks the walk is the right sort of commemoration.

"Oh yah," he says and then changes the subject. We stop at a fork in the path, and he points out the boulders that have been piled along the shore. Burt tells me that the boulders were brought not that long ago, when there was some concern about erosion on the flats. "There's none here to speak of," he tells me. "There never was along the shore here."

As we move along the waterside, Burt tells me about the first time he heard of Lowry's beach life.

"Around the time *Under the Volcano* appeared, I had a friend whose parents had a shack a little west of the Lowrys. He invited me down one day to have a swim and dinner, and we walked along the beach. The tide was out, and we got to this place where we heard this noise. Well, you know, windup phonographs will only go so loud, but there was one of those going, and a lot of chat and some banging on the floor. I asked my friend, 'What's that?' And he said, 'That's some drunken writer called Lowry.'"

Burt directs me along another path, which he says will take us "down to the Lowrys." We pass a set of concrete steps leading to a boulder on the beach that is meant to mark the original shack's site. I ask if the walk has marked the correct spot. Burt, for the first time engaged with the question of suitable commemoration, answers confidently.

"No, it's not," he says with a knock of his walking stick on the ground and goes on to tell me that one of the organizers of the Lowry Walk admitted to him after the fact that she wasn't sure where the shack had been, so she took a guess. We walk about forty-five paces east to where the shack actually stood. Burt points out the indentation in the ground where Margerie kept a flower garden, and he is amused by the fact that the Parks Board has run a drainage pipe through exactly the spot where the Lowry shack stood.

"But it doesn't matter much, this kind of thing," he tells me. "It's not as though Allah's going to appear here."

Throughout our walk I've been carefully avoiding any direct questions about Lowry, trying in my overly polite way to honour the tenor of Burt's letter to me and his frustration with writers who come to fish around in his past. I direct the conversation to subjects like the freighter out in the inlet or a venerable-looking stump until Burt cannot take my evasive tactics any longer and tells me the story of his first meeting with the Lowrys.

"Dorothy and I were looking for a place to escape, and I thought of the squatters' places down in Cates Park. We went down to the beach and came across this decrepit shack. A lot of these places were built on pilings, above the high-tide line, so when the tide came in, it just went under the house and the deck if there was one. I went up the steps of this place, and Margerie must have seen us from their place. She came out onto the pier and said, 'Ahoy, you chaps, that place is dangerous.' So I backed off and we went over to the Lowrys, which was right next door. We told her what we were looking for, and at that moment we were standing on the deck, and out of the doorway comes Malcolm Lowry. He's dressed in shorts and a plaid shirt, and he has a little stub of a pencil in his fist. I said, 'My God, you're Malcolm Lowry. I'd like to shake your hand. I've got your book.' And he said, 'So you're the guy who bought it.'"

Burt goes on to tell me about the shack the Lowrys helped him buy, of Margerie's reliance on him and Dorothy for company and of some of his duties caring for the shack after they left.

"Next to the Lowry's shack was a little abandoned structure nicknamed the mink house after its regular tenant. The Lowrys owned the building," Burt explains. "That's where they stored a lot of the stuff they didn't want. I was in there two or three times. It was mostly *Life* magazines, *Time* and *Liberty*. But there were manuscripts in there too," Burt says. "They were all soaking wet. He was unsuccessful at the time. And no hope. All those manuscripts had been looked at by Marjerie, and she decided they weren't valuable. That stuff just stayed where it was."

I imagine piles of discarded manuscripts tied with the thick, soft twine that's only found nowadays in your grandmother's kitchen drawer. Think of all the ghost-narratives shuttling about in the shadows. Versions discarded and bequeathed to the mink as bedding for wet winter nights.

ON THE WEST SIDE of Cates Park is a broad expanse of hill and grass that predates the landscaped pathway named for Lowry. On display is a weird array of objects with little relationship to one another, a kind of outdoor version of the curiosity cabinets beloved of Victorian collectors. There is

The calm waters and little-visited beach of Dollarton's foreshore flats

an old anchor that was donated by the Cates family. A pockmarked cement sculpture of a seal sits on a pedestal. There is a brick concession stand, inexplicably closed, and a big parking lot. Two totem poles seem to grow out of the grass, and inside a cedar and mesh structure the size of a large garage sits a war canoe, vintage 1920, which was carved, a plaque informs passersby, by Chief Peter George of the Burrard Band. The canoe is a token of the substantial marine traffic that once moved between the major Squamish settlements on both sides of the Burrard Inlet.

On the north shore, the largest village, *Homulcheson*, was just east of where the Lion's Gate now sets its giant iron foot on the land. Farther east, near the centre of what is now North Vancouver, was *Ustlawn*, or *Slawn*, as some Squamish called it. Today these sites would be no more than twenty minutes from Dollarton by car. Back across the inlet was *Snauq*, where the foot of the Burrard Bridge is now; *A-yuo-shun* at English Bay; *Chay-Hoos* at Prospect Point; *E-yal-mough*, where the Jericho Beach sailing centre is today. At the spot we call Lumberman's Arch in Stanley Park was a large and ancient village known as *Whoi-*

Whoi. When Captain George Vancouver sailed into the inlet in 1792, he saw huge cedar slab houses. Of this early morning sail he wrote, "Here we were met by about fifty Indians in canoes, Who conducted themselves with great decorum and civility, presenting us with several fish cooked and undressed of a sort resembling smelt."

Though Vancouver and his men were mesmerized by the canoes full of Squamish who greeted their arrival, his journal reports that as he passed through the inlet he saw no other villages on either shore. Since the Squamish villages were set back from the beaches, hidden by the towering forest that grew almost to the water's edge, they went unremarked.

The Squamish are invisible in Lowry's version of Dollarton. By the time he arrived on the beach, most of their villages, fishing grounds and cemeteries had been obliterated, and much of the native population had been gathered onto reserves that dot the North Shore. In the thousands of pages Lowry wrote during the years he lived at Dollarton, references to native culture are remarkably rare. Without acknowledging the sudden replacement of Squamish villages by a burgeoning European-settled cosmopolis, Lowry did note that the pace of subdivision around Dollarton was slowed as developers found themselves "baffled by the Indian reserve." The Squamish coastal landscape, with its network of villages, its massive cedar meeting houses and its busy canoe traffic, did not exist for Lowry. Its markings on the coast had been so thoroughly forgotten, rubbed out, that they had been rendered unreadable.

But we shouldn't forget how deeply unfashionable it was in Lowry's day to concern oneself with the demolition of native culture. It is our political concerns, our historical hindsight, as well as an uneasy guilt, that make Lowry an easy mark as we point to his ignorance of Dollarton's deep First Nations history.

I LEARN ABOUT NATIVE SETTLEMENT along the Burrard Inlet, along with a few words of Squamish, from Major James Skitt Matthews, b. Newton, North Wales, Sept. 1878; Archivist City of Vancouver. Matthews was as careful a recorder of local history as the inlet has seen. He made intricate lists of Squamish place names and landmarks, catalogued the names of as many inhabitants of these villages as he could and interviewed numerous Squamish and pioneers who did business with them or married into the local tribes. Matthews' primary archival method looks quaintly archaic to the contemporary eye, considering our dedication to storing material away in the dark circuitry of a laptop's hard drive. Working with index cards, he collected a hodgepodge of material that he gathered from a range of sources: newspapers, interviews, photographs in the city archive's collection, bits and pieces from books and pamphlets that he clipped and glued to his cards.

One card, titled "Dollarton, North Arm, Burrard Inlet," offers a typical example of Matthews' method. Typed on the left-hand side of the card, in the still-familiar though now antique-looking letters of a manual Underwood, is the following:

card three
Capt. Chas. W. Cates told me about Aug. 20th 1952, that the Indians tell him the name for Dollarton in Squamish is "SEE-MAM-ETTE", or "SAY-MAM-ET" because the Indians used to send their lazy people there; people who would not work.

The care with dates and proper transliteration of Squamish words is characteristic of Matthews' cards, as is the care with which he hunted down and carefully culled the local lore that old-timers had to offer. Matthews' informant, Capt. Chas. W. Cates, an ex-North Vancouver mayor who wrote a book on local tides and was an authority on native lore, happens to be the son of the man for whom Cates Park was named.

But Matthews' best informant on the Squamish landscape of the North Shore prior to European settlement was August Jack Khahtsahlano. Born at the False Creek Reserve in 1877, the grandson of a chief, Khahtsahlano's family gave its name to Kitsilano, Vancouver's gracious west-side neighbourhood. One of the commonplace stories told about August Jack places him on Kitsilano Beach, digging unsuccessfully for gold believed to have been buried there by his ancestors before they were removed to make way for the city's movement west.

Between 1932 and 1954 Matthews carried on numerous conversations with Khahtsahlano, sometimes in the archive's office at Vancouver City Hall or afloat on a steamer in the inlet so Khahtsahlano could point to abandoned village sites and landmarks as they sailed through the country that August Jack's ancestors knew as *Sko-mish-oath*.

The two men seem to have had a lively friendship. August Jack often brought a paper bag full of artifacts to Matthews' office for the archivist to admire. One of the discomforting aspects of Matthews' jaunty response to these offerings was his habit of ending a meeting by offering August Jack a few bucks in exchange for a canoe oar or a goat-hair blanket. On one occasion Matthews paid fifty dollars and twenty dollars for two ancestral masks that ended up on display in a large glass show case in the city archives.

The most striking meetings between these two men—each representative of a vastly different way of life on the shores of Burrard Inlet—took place at Matthews' Arbutus Street home, near the University of British Columbia endowment lands on Vancouver's west side, where he lived for many years. We can imagine the handsome mock-tudor bungalow faced in stucco, windows with leaded panes, the lush green yard and the back patio circled by hydrangeas and tulips, the nostalgic greenery of British gardens that still makes up a good part of Vancouver's summer wealth. August Jack, who lives with his wife on the Capilano Indian Reserve, comes calling with his paper bag full of heirlooms. And Matthews, the native of Montgomeryshire and ever the archivist, records every word they share after his guest has left. These jottings he will later hand over to his typist. Matthews describes the two of them, "one white, one brown," sitting "on a cottage veranda one sunny summer's evening . . . old friends, enjoying each other's company" with a tray of tea and iced cake between them. Matthews jokes with August Jack, calling him a Stone Age man, while Khahtsahlano gets the better of his host, calling him a relief age man. It is 1937 and Khahtsahlano is appalled at the white man's inability to feed, house and find work for the Depression poor.

As August Jack describes early life on the inlet, partly from memory, partly through stories passed down to him by elders, he brings a whole other world into view; *Sko-mish-oath* takes shape like a dream seen through Alice's fabled looking glass. He tells of men spearing whales off Brockton Point, which is now a traffic turnaround in Stanley Park; he tells of *Homulcheson,* the village just east of the Capilano River, near Dollarton, where cedar meeting houses sixty to eighty feet long stood hidden among the crab apple trees. When asked how many Squamish lived around Burrard Inlet before the coming of Europeans, Khahtsahlano cannily announces, "About a million!" And soon enough the two men revert to the bizarre jokes they habitually share, which are destined to be set out by Matthews' typist in what looks like an amateur screenplay scenario:

> Major Matthews: "Good gracious! What's happened to your hands? They're whiter than mine. What have you been doing to them?"
>
> August: "Been using too much whiteman's soap, I guess, and washed all the colour out."

These bantering meetings carried on well into the 1950s while Lowry, one can imagine, was chopping wood in his Dollarton paradise. Having kidded each other and made the day's polite transaction, Matthews would give the man he calls "one of nature's gentleman" a dollar and a quarter to get his wife a present. Then, the archivist and the grandson of a Squamish chief would sit in silence as the evening golds and greens gathered in the bottoms of their English bone teacups.

IT'S OFTEN SAID that Canadians have no heroes, that we refuse to revere our political leaders the way the Americans do or love our artists and writers in the style of the Europeans. Lowry's life (and the afterlife his notoriety and fame brought him) is no exception. After he'd published his one indisputably important book, journalists came to Dollarton, not to honour this literary Caesar of the season, but to belittle him as King of the beach squatters who could write a cheque for thousands while living tax free on public land. Aside from a few aficionados (Dylan Thomas was among Lowry's admirers) and university students who sought Lowry out because of the fame of his novel, most of the attention he received came in the form of eviction notices.

For some reason, Lowry took these threats by the city to bulldoze his shack into the sea far more seriously than many of the other squatters, including Harvey Burt, who scoffs at the Lowrys' misguided decision to abandon their shack in 1954 while others held on for another decade and a half. In 1971, when the last of the shacks along the flats were bulldozed, their ruins set ablaze, bits of antique gingerbread trim were saved and carted off to be donated to the Vancouver Museum, but little else remains as a memento of the beach shacks that existed, like a cut-rate version of Venice, along one of the country's busiest waterways for nearly twenty-five years.

The appearance of the Malcolm Lowry Walk in the late 1980s, commemorating a bit of British Columbia that had been consciously and rather brutally obliterated, seems characteristic of Western Canadian development. In boom times, heritage deemed too recent a vintage to be of value is demolished. Then, in hindsight, in soberer times, we look back at what we've done and try to make amends.

The shacks at Dollarton are irrevocably gone. And when I walk along the water's edge on the neatly landscaped forest path named for the author of *Under the Volcano*, I imagine an alternate outcome: one shack (it could be the Lowrys' or the Burts' or just any four-square, dry-in-the-rain unit) is preserved as an authentic relic of squatter life on the beach. Instead of the boulder that sits on the flats in mute commemoration, the shack stands still on its piles over the foreshore rocks. It is well preserved, like a beloved old convertible or a family photo album. Young writers apply to the Canada Council or the North Shore Council or the Lowry

Council—whichever council wants the work—for a fellowship that supports a few months' stay in the shack as a writer's retreat. The shithouse would be rebuilt—this time in a more suitable spot, since, Burt tells me, that the Lowry's latrine was placed uphill on a spot where it likely fouled the spring they took their water from. The toughest candidates could live and work in the shack through Vancouver's grey, wet winter, filling the wood stove and watching the forest turn to crystal. Sun-worshippers among the applicants could request a term from July to October, when the mixture of coastal sun and leaf and calm are a true balm to the soul. In this scenario the Malcolm Lowry Walk has a future and not just a past, and the question of whether Lowry is a Canadian hero or not would be moot.

But even when a visitor to the Dollarton area has given up such daydreams, the shore of the Burrard Inlet still inspires. It is treed and gulls float placidly in the wake of passing boats. The beach is rough and rocky with twisted crab legs stuck in wet crevices. If you stop and listen carefully, the sound of the beach mud and stones drying out can be heard as water runs off toward the inlet in the last sigh of the retreating tide.

The last time I was on the beach, the wooden platform that is meant to honour Lowry was covered with the leavings of a previous night's party: one empty bottle of Fruitopia; one empty bottle of Squirt; one empty bottle of Cuerva Especial Tequila; two empty packets of Marlboros; two spent candles, one purple, the other white, poked into cracks in the platform's planking and burned down to the size of a bottle cap. These things made me wonder if someone had been up to some kind of devotions the night before. But the odds were good that these things had nothing to do with Lowry. They were more likely the leftovers of a more generally practiced Canadian ritual: teenage sex in the outdoors.

Still, the bottles, candles and Marlboro boxes reminded me of the mess I'd seen near the tomb of Jim Morrison in the famous Parisian cemetery of Père La-Chaise. There I saw well-dressed European tourists being shoed away by a drunken cemetery guard, and second-generation hippie chicks, their boyfriends wearing their guitars hung rakishly over

Leavings at the commemoration meant to mark Lowry's years at Dollarton

their backs on a piece of twine. I was told that the area around Morrison's grave had been more or less cleaned up from what had been its totally chaotic state a few years before, when graffiti and incense and garbage had covered all the neighbouring tombs as well as Morrison's. With the site's new orderliness, the worshippers on the margins would have to move on to some new shrine—the sidewalk in Los Angeles where River Phoenix collapsed and died or Kurt Cobain's suicide mansion. In the same way, people will keep moving to the margins of B.C. life, only to be removed as their hideout gets written into someone's development plan.

A fight similar to the one that festered over the Dollarton Flats has been brewing between squatters and the government on the south coast of Vancouver Island. At Sombreo Beach, which overlooks Juan de Fuca Straight a few miles from the logging town of Port Renfrew, a small group of long-time residents, surfers and more or less checked-out ex-hippies has been hoping against hope that their little paradise at the edge of the continent will not be turned into another of B.C.'s remarkable parks. Some of the squatters at Sombreo came from the long beaches up island near Tofino, when Pacific Rim National Park was created in the 1970s. Approximately a dozen cabins, built of driftwood and plywood and often wrapped in plastic to ward off the rain, stand at Sombreo, not in the shadow of old growth, but alongside a buffer of forest left when the area inland was logged in the mid-1990s. Like all squatters, the people at Sombreo Beach chose to build their homes beyond the reach of the long arm of officialdom and land title searches. But their flight from mainstream Canadian life does not necessarily make them heroes or suited to chronicle their habitat's demise. A friend of mine who visited Sombreo wrote to me of a distinctly unheroic fellow who believed aliens were speaking to him though his chimney. To prove it, he invited my friend to listen to the wind whistling down his stove pipe. In time, these squatters will be moved along, just as Malcolm Lowry gave up his beloved oasis.

It's all a jumble down at Cates Park, though an officially sanctioned jumble—a gathering of totems, deep-sea anchors, a boat launch, the plaque dedicated by the city to its most famous squatter. But it may be that among all the park's clutter and haphazard mementoes it's still possible to imagine the version of Dollarton each one of us prefers, to choose between Squamish fishing grounds, millwright's work site, a reclusive writer's oasis, or—admitting the inevitable—a good spot to walk the dog.

Mapping the Boom and Bust

A s I write, Calgary is in the grip of another boom. The production policies of oil sheiks in faraway Saudi Arabia have lifted oil prices to a record thirty dollars a barrel, and demand in the United States for Canadian natural gas has skyrocketed. With the resulting windfall, the Alberta government has announced its willingness to reinvest in the social services it gradually opted out of when the last boom went bust. I remember bumper stickers and T-shirts that pleaded, "Please Lord, Let There Be One More Oil Boom and I Promise I Won't Piss It Away." Not eloquent, but an honest plea. In the lead-up to the present prosperity, however, Albertans were reminded that they are not that different from everyone else. Their hospitals became overfilled, schools went downhill and homelessness proved to be part of prairie living, not a specialty of big Eastern cities. In Calgary, homelessness has its own twist: there are the traditional down-and-outers, with no work or family or place to sleep, but the recent boom also has created a caste known as the working homeless, who have jobs, but can't find an affordable place to live in the overheated economy.

When I was a teenager, in the middle seventies, the idea of large numbers of homeless people on Calgary's streets would have struck most people as unlikely—a big city problem. I do remember one: a most unusual figure who haunted the downtown alleyways with a bag to scavenge found objects from garbage dumpsters. She had one outfit that gave her an unintentional punk stylishness—a cape of black felt worn over tights and rubber boots, along with wrap-around dark glasses and a flock of silver barrettes in her kinky hair. I never heard her speak, but the look she gave me on a late afternoon in the shade of an old brick office block told me to keep my distance. So I did. I think of this woman now as a kind of ghost out of Calgary's past. A lurking apparition, she symbolized the unlikeliness or at least the hiddenness of the poor in a boom town.

Like this shadow of the past, the stories of my father and his father convey the meaning of Calgary's boom and bust cycles for the people who ride them. Both men are gone, along with the Calgary they knew, which was swept away in consecutive waves of prosperity and failure. If you don't know Calgary, you'll soon get the picture—that prosperity, the dream of the mystical boom that won't go bust, has its own costs.

When my dad collapsed and died of a heart attack on a hot July afternoon sixteen years ago, you could say the Calgary economy finally killed him. Now of course, things were more complicated than that, but the absolutely unpredictable course of his success and descent in the local boom and bust cycles went a long way toward knocking him out of the game. If you had met a week or two before he died, you would have seen a man in his midsixties, just starting to show his age. His hair combed back from his forehead and the sides of his head in the way men of his generation favoured. An expressive face, playful lines about the eyes and a bud of a smile beneath a big Russian nose. A man made in a time that valued food above exercise, suburban living above city buzz, work above travel.

The week after my father's death, I went to his office to clean out his desk and made a surprising discovery. Along with the things I expected to find—neatly arranged Visa slips, mortgage records, a copy of Fowler's *English Usage* (my father, as someone put it, was an old-fashioned, educated businessman)—I came across a pile of postcards. I'd never known my dad to be a collector of anything. He'd given up his stamp collection as a twelve-year-old, and he hadn't taken or pasted a photograph in an album in decades. The postcards were of two kinds: they included portraits of entertainers he'd loved: the Marx Brothers and Jackie Gleason raising his "to the moon Alice" fist. But as well, there was a card picturing Calgary, circa 1956, as painted by the West Coast artist E.J. Hughes. Hughes is known for his paintings of fishing boats afloat in B.C. harbours, but apparently he'd visited Calgary in the mid-1950s and set his easel on the North Hill overlooking the Bow River, the downtown and, at a distance, the Rocky Mountains.

This was Calgary as my dad knew it as a young man. A bit of big city feel along the central east–west streets, where buildings above six or eight stories were becoming numerous. But in Hughes' Calgary the Palliser Hotel is still a notable landmark, along with the grey cast-cement silos of the Robin Hood Flour Mill. Along the blocks nearer the river, on streets fanning out from the Centre Street Bridge, stand the old frame houses built in the early decades of the twentieth century. Hughes paints them to look like wooden toys, with square eyelike windows in their grey roof peaks. You can still recognize an orderly residential neighbourhood north of City Hall, with substantial trees—fir, maple and poplar scattered among them—each one, as my dad used to say, planted by hand, since the dry south bank of the Bow was no lush, treed precinct in its natural state.

It was among these houses, slightly to the west of Hughes' view, that my dad grew up, on streets much like the ones the painter presents. And it was on the same streets that he was initiated into the Calgary economy, sitting before school and then again after dinner till midnight, behind the counter of his parents' corner store, which was named, in honour of the nearby military barracks, Mewata Grocery.

Grocery stores provided an opening for newcomers in a small city, where the political establishment and economy was, for the most part, WASP-led. The grocery business allowed not only an economic foothold, but served as a local meeting place. The ubiquitous grocery store often had a soda fountain, some had a coffee shop, and the popular magazines of the day were displayed, so the boys from the Navy would come in and spend the evening flipping through them. In a very Calgarian development, Jewish newcomers took up these kinds of small businesses, while

E.J. Hughes' midfifties watercolour of downtown Calgary and the Centre Street Bridge

their Chinese counterparts tried their luck with corner laundries. The first known Jewish-owned business in the area was a prototypic grocery store run by the Repstein brothers from Winnipeg, who arrived on the first train from the east in August 1883. In a tent, not far from where my dad grew up, they established the Cheap Cash Store, offering dry goods and groceries they'd brought with them from Manitoba.

My grandfather had no great ambitions connected with his grocery business. It supported his family and gave him a degree of personal freedom that he could not have had in Russia. He'd brought his family to Canada in the early twenties, travelling from Europe aboard a steamer called *The Empress of France,* following a few relatives who had preceded him to Calgary. One among these arranged for a farmer named Peter Stokke to give my grandfather work on his farm at the rate of $10 a month, room and board included. It was not enough at that time that a family member sponsor newcomers; work for them on the railroad or in agriculture had to be guaranteed.

If you refer nowadays to Calgary's old Jewish neighbourhood, people look at you as if you've lost your mind. *What old Jewish neighbourhood?* they want to know. And in a way they're right. There hasn't been such a thing in view for decades. But still, there were a few blocks of frame houses and groceries, storefronts and boarding houses, hooked into the southern bank of the Bow River that had a unique character, making up a neighbourhood that would prove to be on the outer western fringe of Calgary's biggest building boom.

Apart from catching the city before that boom, Hughes' painting of a pristine post-war city against the backdrop of a sweet blue sky evokes this and other downtown enclaves before they began to break up. It evokes as well the lostness of such early versions of the city, thrown out with the spring when the autumn of one economic cycle gave way to the excitement of new growth. Hughes may have been thinking of the city's ability to offer the kind of eternal prosperity that most North Americans dreamed of after the war. And by coincidence—perhaps this is why the postcard was preserved—it was in the middle fifties that my father convinced his old-fashioned parents, who were satisfied to go on selling potatoes and ice cream sodas from eight till midnight, to turn their grocery store into a small appliance and furniture store. This, you might say, was a stroke of genius.

Around this time, small family-owned chains of grocery sellers—the early versions of our Safeways and Loblaws—were beginning to make the future of independent grocers look bleak. But more importantly, with the coming prosperity of the oil-supported 1960s (along with befinned Cadillacs, big steaks and Vegas holidays) came sprawling subdivisions with thousands of new homes that needed a full set of appliances and furniture. These were the neighbourhoods where Calgary's growing middle class wanted to live—and with them went the children who had been born in the old downtown, and who came to think of its streets not as home, but rather as grist for the real estate mill.

When my dad talked about his early successful years, in the late 1950s and '60s, he never claimed any special foresight. The money was lying in the street, he said. You had to be an idiot not to pick it up. By the prosperous late sixties, most of the old downtown had been demolished, from solid sandstone office blocks to modest wooden houses. Calgary, the rumour went, was famous in architectural circles for having fewer pre-1960 structures than any other city its age in the world. The old riverside streets, along with most of the city's established downtown, would fall to the wrecker's ball to make way for a new city, a modern city, a more American city (as Texas oilmen got involved in the excitement) and a more troubled city, as events like the 1973 Mideast War and Pierre Trudeau's National Energy Policy flattened prosperity as smoothly as a June hailstorm puts an end to Calgary gardens. Still, once the boom and bust cycle was in motion, it was unstoppable. The years of deflated failure were as assured as the heady decades that followed.

Downtown Calgary, especially the blocks tucked up against the Bow, hides an amazing record of change and disruption. Hughes' painting is breathtaking for the image it presents of an absolutely vanished place. As vanished as any Babylonian suburb on the Tigris. And so, it is in this tiny and oldest part of the city where I go again and again to look for the shadows of the lost cities my father knew.

In fact it was lumber—not cattle and certainly not oil—that supported the first sizeable town site along the southern bank of the Bow. In 1886, roughly five blocks northeast as the crow flies from the corner where my dad had his store and seven blocks from the house where he grew up, an Ontarian named Kerr, who'd made money milling lumber along the Eau Claire River in Wisconsin, built a mill on the Bow's south shore. After securing leases with the federal government for the timber upriver, Kerr began floating felled trees to his mill site, which produced the first steady jobs for workers in the Calgary area, as well as the wood that built the new blocks of two-storey frame houses that began appearing just up from the river bank on First and Second Avenues.

Though my grandfather's house—built for a doctor and not a mill worker—had a design unlike a lot of its neighbours, it was surrounded by rows of shingled, rectangular boxes, with their modest roof peak sheltering a couple bedrooms, a covered veranda out front and a small square plot of grass between the house and the sidewalk. Most of these houses were built from plans bought from American building firms, with slight differences in façade or window arrangement setting one building apart from its neighbour.

As the city grew and construction moved farther south of the river, different types of professional men began building houses for themselves on streets deemed worthy of each guild's unique station. On Third Avenue the firemen and railway men put a block's distance between themselves and the millwrights who'd settled before them. And on Fourth Avenue surgeons and accountants and furriers built more elegant sandstone houses. The doctor who built the house where my dad grew up chose to place his home on Seventh Avenue. This careful layering of residential status, the changing pattern of wood-built to stone-built homes, is gone, as if these men's doings were swept up with the snow one morning.

Somehow, I've come to feel that the way the city has abandoned its past so readily might help me understand the direction of my dad's last years. What did it mean to grow up and work all your life in a city that was constantly remaking itself? How did it feel to establish a business in a neighbourhood where everything familiar vanished but for the odd, sad relic that escaped demolition by chance?

Besides a few photographs, I have very few things that call to mind the house my father grew up in Calgary's downtown before the Second World War. The neighbourhood, like the family grocery, took its name from the Mewata Armouries, a red-brick barn of a place modelled after a Scottish baronial manor. The family home on Seventh Avenue was so close to the grocery store that if my dad had stood on the roof of the house he would have been able to see if customers were coming or going. The house is gone now, a gravel parking lot replacing it a number of years back. It was the kind of stucco and wood home that would be prized in other cities where character buildings stand a chance, but Calgary is not

Precious few of Calgary's early frame houses remain. This one presents its neat façade almost as it would have upon completion.

one of those places. The property on which my grandfather's house sat was swept up in the frenzy of buying that took place in the mid-1970s, when a fencepost and a couple of stones was worth good money to anyone crazy for a stake in the downtown market. Two brothers from Switzerland bought it for an outrageously inflated price, half of which was set aside in trust for an aunt and cousin of mine. But imagine the day that deal went through. A kind of Calgary *Eureka*—like the conquistadors stumbling onto Potosi but without the cruelty. Still, the same dumb luck. If you take a look at the lot today, it doesn't look like it's worth much money. The old picket fence that ringed the house—a foot and a half high—is still in place, as is the corroded sidewalk out front with the metal 1116 set into the cement in front of the gate.

As I pace off the lot—twenty strides wide by thirty-two long—a woman gets out of her car and asks, "What are you doing?"

"This used to be my grandfather's house," I explain, not really answering her question. "My dad grew up here."

"You mean there?" she asks, pointing at the apartment building that appeared on the eastern side of the property in the 1960s. It once contained, on its main floor, a coffee house where, rumour has it, Joni Mitchell played when her name meant nothing and she was rolling from prairie gig to prairie gig.

"No." I point at the lot where she has just paid to park her car. "Here."

"So what are you doing?"

I say something about trying to recover a sense of the neighbourhood where my dad was a young man.

"What's your name?" she asks.

Once I've told her my family name, she is interested and names an uncle of mine, thinking that he might be my dad.

"No," I tell her, "that's my dad's brother."

"Because I grew up just over on Eighth Avenue. Your uncle and I went to McDougall School together."

"Well, my dad was a generation older."

"But your uncle would know me."

And off she goes, no longer spooked by my seemingly pointless pacing. Somewhere nearby there's a twenty by thirty-five foot rectangle of gravel where she might be able to mark out where her girlhood room hung in the air above the lilac bushes.

In 1920, when houses like my grandfather's were new, they had an assessed worth of about eight hundred dollars. Fifteen years later the city's assessor's department put the value of the land and house in the range of five thousand dollars. Like its neighbours its particulars for the purpose of assessment were as follows:

Foundation—concrete
Basement—full
Basement floor—concrete
Exterior walls—stucco

Floors—fir and oak
Construction—fair
Bathrooms—1
Chimneys—1
Roof—shingles
Fuel—gas

All of this was filled in carefully on yellow filing cards preserved at City Hall, in the assessor's neatly curving script, a catalogue of what Calgary builders deemed a modest but comfortable family home in 1920s.

By the time I got to know the house my dad grew up in, my grandfather, long retired, lived there alone. A man who'd served in the Russian army, lived in a wood hut in the Russian hinterland after his family had been banished from Moscow with the rest of its Jews, he now read his newspaper in the sunny front room of his home day in and day out. Widowed in the 1970s, he was left to his weekend synagogue visits and his household chores. The house at 1116 – 7th Avenue had seen better days, but it still had its charms. Like nearly every old Calgary house, it had lilacs in the yard and a runner of lily of the valley along the shady eastern wall. There were built-in cabinets in the dining room with leaded, inlaid glass. In the kitchen nook there was just enough room for the wooden benches some crafty carpenter had built against the walls and the table surface, like a heavy picnic table, fastened to solid feet fixed to the floor.

The living room was dark. My grandmother—we called her granny, though her husband wore the Old World moniker of *zaida*—had put up oversized green and white metal awnings to keep the sun off her chintz and tasseled sofa cushions. A gold framed oil painting hung over the mantel, which showed a scene from some French romance: a big pompadoured woman in a flowing, striped dress, who lounged, one gold-shoed foot extended, as she oversaw a child's piano practice. Like all things encountered in childhood that seem out of place, I assumed there was something about this painting that related to my grandparents' otherwise modest surroundings that I simply couldn't fathom. God knows where they got it, and who knows into whose hands it went. I suppose it was the green in the dress that caught my grandmother's eye or the idea that the portrait was European in a classy way. The right kind of European, that is. Not the kind of European that she was and no longer wanted to be.

Like all old houses, 1116 – 7th Avenue had its share of oddities that put a mixture of fear and excitement into a child's heart. There were two particularly scare-worthy features that fascinated my brother and me. One was the stairway leading up to the bedrooms on the second floor, where my uncle and aunt had their rooms as kids. We found an old defunct Singer sewing machine up there, surrounded by a lethal-looking array of half unspun spools, needles and elastic for skirt waists. The machine had the same melancholy effect as a car wrecked and left to rust in a field. It suggested the turning point in someone's youth, my aunt's most likely, but maybe my grandmother's, when one of them had given up on the difficult work of making and mending clothes. I could imagine the last time someone took a pattern up there, and patiently saw the project through to its end. The Singer was my version of Mrs. Havisham's mouldy wedding cake. It conjured everything that was unknown about adult life for a ten-year-old, and it provided a reminder of the impossibility of knowing what one's elders were really like when they were young. In some subtler way, the machine seemed a sign of some mysterious, creeping unhappiness. Its abandonment at the top of the stairs made me think, for no reason I could explain, of other disappointments. It gave me a faint sense that nothing in life was guaranteed.

The other ghostly seeming stairway in my grandfather's house led from the kitchen down past a cluttered broom closet to the basement. Its steps were small, covered in green linoleum and made a couple quick bends so the descent was like going below on a battleship. A bare bulb lit the way to the bottom, where a tiny cellar under the stairs was always full of what seemed to me to be hundreds of cans of apple sauce and corn and peas. The neat lines of tins must have given my grandfather pleasure, reminding him of his first and last career in Calgary as the proprietor of Mewata Grocery.

But the strange lightless gathering of tins gave me a funny feeling too. It had the same effect on me as my grandfather's habit of saving every bit of string, every wax paper bag that came into his kitchen.

To a youth these fussy domestic doings always seem crazed and unnecessary. There are always more wax paper bags coming, aren't there? But then we all hit an age when we start to do these things ourselves.

Two more oddities in the old house fascinated us as kids. Neither of them was scare-worthy, but both seemed to be things out of a fairy tale or fable. One of these was a sloping storm cellar door set in the ground in the backyard. You opened it by lifting it away from the concrete frame to step onto the stairs that led to the basement. To me this was pure Kansas, comic protection against tornadoes that never arrived on our prairies. The door had a rusty old keyhole you could look through. And when we were finished climbing on it and using it as a slide, we would thrill to the act of lifting it away from where it lay and looking down into the cool light filtering through the loose cement dust.

The other object that fascinated us was an old clock in a dark wood cabinet that had the face and chimes of a grandfather clock but was only a few feet high and hung on the wall. My grandfather would lift two dainty pins to unlatch its glass face and then use a key that lay hidden behind the clock's mechanism to wind it, so that always, under his steady care, it kept perfect Calgary time.

My memories of visits to the house where my dad grew up are few but strong. On Sundays when I was in my early teens, my dad and I would put the electric mower in the trunk of his blue Buick and go over to cut my grandfather's grass. The house was too old to have outdoor outlets, so you had to run the cord through an open window or the front door and plug it into the living room wall, not far from the painted lady with the green dress. My grandfather, then in his eighties, would come out in his shirt sleeves with a pair of clippers. As I motored around in the dust, kicking up the appley scent of a weed I haven't encountered since, my grandfather clipped the edges of his yard, along the greying picket fence and the relatively plantless garden beds. What a strange homesteading bunch we were, kicking up the prairie sand, surrounded by parking lots where neighbouring buildings had already been flipped and torn down in a dream of future development fortunes.

When the job was finished, we sat beside the old sparkling white stove at the kind of arborite and chrome kitchen table that is back in style, drinking ginger ale and eating neapolitan ice cream from mismatched bowls. My grandmother had been dead a few years by then, and the thought of my grandfather offering us this domestic treat more or less breaks my heart when I think about it now. I marvel at the order in his old man's days. His clean shirts, the stack of white undershirts I once saw on the corner of his bed, the neatness of his newspaper when he finished reading it. The care with which he wound the old wall clock.

My dad's success was part of the big post-war boom that I was lucky enough to be born into. His success erased my grandfather's immigrant city—a city of millwrights and corner stores—and made way for my generation, which rarely thought about the past. Why would it? The past had nothing to do with the promise of prosperity, which rode the evening breeze with the scent of grilling sirloin and the perfume of lush lawn cut and bagged.

Still, I did catch a glimpse of the risk involved in riding the wave of Calgary's boom. As the 1970s came on, my dad's furniture business was being challenged by the big discounters like The Brick. Boom business arrived at his door one final time, when the city's plans for a northwest Light Rail Transit line made a part of the property his store sat on necessary for the train's right of way along Tenth Street. Public transit was not an immediately popular idea, as Albertans, like Californians, are wedded to the idea of their cars as personal freedom machines. But the boom had brought sprawl to the city, and sprawl meant worsening traffic problems. The city proposed expropriating a half block of frontage at the western edge of the downtown on the corner of Sixthth Avenue and Tenth Street, where the original grocery store had stood. By the time the city came calling, the original corner block was a one-storey adjunct to the main five-storey building.

Ravvin's Furniture, the building partly amputated by City expropriation for LRT right of way, near the bend in the Bow River where Calgary's town site was initiated

But there was one obstacle to the LRT sale. Just over the Louise Bridge on the other side of the Bow River were the old neighbourhoods of Sunnyside and Hillhurst. There, the elderly owners of wood-frame houses and modest lots were attracting a good deal of attention from press and politicians alike. This was not a heritage issue or a preservation issue. Those words didn't exist in Calgary twenty-five years ago any more than we had palm trees growing along the roadside. The residents of Hillhurst–Sunnyside did not want a Light Rail line running through their backyards. They did not care about the inflated boom-time compensation the city was willing to pay for their property. They wanted their homes just as they had always been: quiet, valued not for their flippability, but in visits from children to the front porch and the fullness of their gardens in August.

This fight between city expropriators and old-timers gave me my first lesson in civic politics, civic bumbling and that hurting feeling in the gut that follows a missed opportunity. It marked, as well, a turning point in

Calgary's fortunes. My memory of the elderly ladies of Sunnyside and their distracted-looking husbands is quite clear. I saw them first in their numbers at a city council meeting. I also remember how my dad looked, sitting at a distance in the council chambers because he'd arrived earlier than I had; he resembled a fighter who'd been tired out by his opponent. And I remember Ross Alger, the mayor who presided over this gathering, only in silhouette: a dark suit, a bland, middle-aged face, hair slicked back the way men hadn't done for thirty years.

The mayor was careful not to play his hand. He was pro-development, but he didn't want to lose every vote to be had among the Sunnyside rate-payers. He barely moved in his chair as he followed the pointer a city consultant waved in front of a neighbourhood map projected on a screen. In the centre of the map was the corner under discussion, where the first leg of track would run alongside the Louise Bridge, over the river on its way north. The land sat at one of the base points of the neat triangle that made up the earliest area of settlement on the Calgary town site.

Less than a hundred years before, Blackfoot had camped out there, keeping a wary distance from the whiteman's fort, but drawn inevitably by the opportunities for trade. In those early days no bridge existed for crossings to the north side of the river, where one day the houses of Hillhurst and Sunnyside would stand. A private ferry ran people across for a few cents. When the river flooded, women took their children shopping in rowboats.

But none of this mattered as differing interests argued over the future of what was now prime real estate snuggled into the elbow of the Bow River. If things went in my dad's favour, the rear of his store—a glassed-in, boxy space where he showcased broadloom—would go the way of all things, along with a little booze can called Ten Foot Henrys that nestled against the back wall of the store in a building owned by another Calgarian hoping his pot of gold had arrived.

When the meeting was over, the mayor's councillors hadn't managed to settle their differences. It was somehow clear that the elderly ladies of Sunnyside would get their way, at least for the time being. This was an amazing and possibly unique occurrence in the history of downtown Calgary. The rush of newness, of constant transformation and growth was blocked by sentiment, by the tenacious rootedness of elders who stood for votes before a mayor who wanted to appear even-handed.

A few years later the Light Rail, dubbed the C Train, went through as planned. The line had the same effects it would have had on Sunnyside when it was first proposed. Laying tracks for an electric train leaves none of the devastation caused by the digging of subway tunnels. The key difference, however, was that the corner on which my grandfather had first sold potatoes, ice cream and tobacco from behind the counter of the Mewata Grocery was bought by the city at post-boom prices. By the time the deal was settled, the federal government's energy policy had sent Albertan oilmen to Texas to try their luck in a different climate. Head offices had fled the city, leaving hundreds of thousands of seemingly worthless square feet of office space. The husks of half-built buildings squatted not far from the corner at Sixth Avenue and Tenth Street. One of these stood, its concrete skeleton a monument to the passing boom, until not that long ago.

Ross ALGER was an early political player in my view of boom town. Now, he's forgotten totally. He was the mayor during part of my fortunate youth who presided over a turning point that signalled harsher times to come.

By coincidence, I met another mayor of Calgary, Rod Sykes, who presided over the beginning of the city's economic boom in the 1960s. I must have been nine or ten at the time. A neighbour and I had constructed a two—count 'em two—storey fort using the stone retaining wall at the side of our house as a main floor foundation, topping that with a structure of firewood posts and cedar planks. We used the pieces of firewood as corner posts and lay a plank from one log to the next to create a frame. Planking formed the outside walls and firmed up the unsteady structure. On top of everything, we hammered down a roof with a hatch in it for courageous roof sitters. Inside, we placed scraps of shag rug that had come home from the broadloom display at the corner of Sixth and Tenth. I don't remember much of what we did in the fort once it was done. It was full, I think, of comic books, and it was the sort of thing that let you lord over other kids. If you didn't want to let them up for a look, you could just sit on top of the opening that let visitors inside, chewing your Bazooka Joe bubble gum and tell them, "NO. GET OFF MY PROPERTY!"

My partner in this early stab at construction had a well-known father, an old-timer in town who was a higher up in the Reserve Army. Now and again he and his wife had parties to which long black cars would pull up, little flags flying on their fenders. The drivers would hop out and scoot around back of the car to open a door for their illustrious passengers. Out of one of these cars stepped Rod Sykes. He came up my neighbour's driveway—I remember a lean man, out-of-date black suit, almost no hair on a tiny head—and stopped when he saw the daughter of his host peering out of the roof hatch of our little addition to the Calgary real estate scene. He complimented us on its sturdy appearance, and then off he went to martinis and small talk. The mayor of boom town had complimented our industriousness. Had he imagined us playing some childish part in the city's ever-burgeoning growth?

I must give my dad credit for his complete lack of Archie Bunkerish raving about the elderly ladies who'd scuttled the city's original plan. It was as if he recognized the shadow they threw of a forgotten Calgary, a little leftover accent of his father's modest, hard-working city. But the calm with which he simply let it go may well have been an outward sign of inner desperation. I can't say if my father's outward success actually made him happy. Or I should say, I know it didn't make him happy enough. But there was no denying the brokenness that lurked at the heart of my dad's world. Eventually, a wrecked economy would force him to close the store. Shortly before I left for university, he and I went to the store—now a big, nearly empty husk—to see if there might be a desk I could take with me to Vancouver. Nothing we saw fit the bill. Instead, I unhitched one of the oval wooden signs that marked the stairway on each showroom floor. He didn't say a word as I shouldered the blue on white board that read "More Fine Furniture on the Fifth Floor."

Once the store was gone, my father tried other things—a mortgage company, real estate ventures—but nothing that meant what the store had to him. Now, with hindsight, I would say that none of these things grounded him as the store had, none of these second acts could be traced back to the first potato, the first ice cream soda, the first Coke he'd fished out of the grocery store's ice water cooler and opened when a friend came in on the way to school. When times went really sour and people started walking away on third mortgages he'd written, leaving him with the title to odd little unsellable suburban houses, his days as a businessman were numbered. His good humour, his good intentions, his straight-ahead exuberance seemed to get squeezed out of him. In the same way that good times had turned him into a man anyone would like, bad times and bad luck turned him into someone who couldn't abide himself, and he went inward, till you couldn't reach him at all. He had all the trappings of a successful life, but something was missing.

In a way, the relative fleetingness—a couple decades long—of his success is very Calgarian. In a city where only the sturdiest, the most august structures are granted an unbothered old age, he was knocked down the way so many buildings and landmarks have been in the haste to put up something new.

I've lived far from Calgary for many years. Somehow, the course of my dad's luck there made it impossible for me to make a home in the city. And the longer you stay away, the more you feel, upon returning, that the city you knew is gone.

Parking lots and a pool hall are all that's left of my father's life and businesses in the downtown core. Just as I must make do with a pilgrimage to 1116 – 7th Avenue to pace off a gravel lot, I find myself shooting a game of pool at Sunset Billiards, where the big tables are laid out in lines on the main floor of what was my dad's furniture store. There's a little darkened video arcade where his office was, and the cashier where you buy pop and chips or pay for your time on the tables is set up where once a glass counter stood, full of radios and kitchen appliances. Loss leaders, my dad explained, things you sold at a loss to bring people into the store.

*Commemoration of the Old
West amidst insurance and
banking towers*

At eleven o'clock on a bright morning, I find one customer shooting pool by himself amidst the expanse of green felt. No one stands behind the counter where Cheesies and peanuts hang on a rack. I walk through to the big set of stairs at the back of the building that lead to the upper floors. But a new locked gate of metal mesh bars entry.

Out in the lot where the manager has gone to smoke a cigarette I ask what's on the building's upper floors.

"City," he says, flicking his ashes on the tarmac where my dad once parked his car. The man furrows his brow and runs his free hand through his greying crew cut. "City owns the building. Firemen and policemen come here to get their uniforms."

He could not seem less interested when I tell him that the building was originally my dad's furniture store. It's not a past that matters to him.

"You do a good business here?" I ask.

At first he says yes, but adds, "Not now. You know. Summer and holidays. But we're open until three. Five a.m. on weekends."

"You're busy that late?"

"Sure. Sometime you have to kick them out."

"Who comes to play?"

"Office guys, you know."

He pauses for another drag. I point out where my dad's office was. I ask about an old service elevator, which had a door that opened at both its back and front. When I worked during the summer as a stock clerk at the store, we'd loaded sofas and dining room tables onto that thing to take them down to the shipping room. The backbreakers were the sofa beds. But as far as he knows there's no access to an elevator from the billiard hall. He tells me his name is Mike.

"A friend got fired," he adds, "so I got this job."

Later in the day, after my chat with Mike, who seems to have inherited the job of managing Sunset Billiards the way some people inherit a relative's old clothes, I go back with a friend to shoot a game of pool. They don't serve liquor at Sunset Billiards, so the hard-core billiard people must go someplace else. Here the clientele is mostly Asian and fresh faced—foursomes of twenty-year-old guys in jeans and T-shirts with cell phones in their pockets, and the odd group of teenage girls smoking cigarettes as they watch each other shoot, eating fast food they've brought in from a nearby 7–Eleven. The players have that lean, spry teenage energy, and from the window table where my friend and I play I look up from each shot to see a choreography of neatly shorn heads bending and rising, elbows pointed with each set-up. There is a constant circling as one player makes way for another around the table.

At about eleven, three teenage girls come in, their midriffs bare, jeans riding low on their hips. They might be fifteen or sixteen. They play a quick game, smiling at each other's shots, then leave. Outside, I see a police car's flashers as a cop waves someone over at the intersection.

The day after my pool game at Sunset Billiards, I meet Harry Sanders out front of the big windows that once showed off my father's sofas and now provide passersby with a theatre of pool hall action. Harry is my age. He's lived in Calgary most of his life, and he has an uncommon obsession for a Calgarian of his generation: he knows a great deal about local history, about the city's architectural heritage and about the transformation the downtown has undergone through drastically unpredictable economic cycles. He weds a scholar's desire to get things right with the popularizer's pleasure at grabbing an audience. And from his work at the City of Calgary Archives, as a columnist on local history for newspapers and the CBC, as well as through his contributions as a consultant to the City's Heritage Advisory Board, Harry probably knows better than anyone the particular way that boom and bust cycles account for the characteristic way Calgarians view themselves and their home town.

When I ask if it's difficult to pursue his interests in a city famous for forgetfulness, Harry begins by answering yes, then switches to a less pessimistic view.

"But things are changing. There's still a lot of ancestor worship: *Look how good the pioneers were who made this great city.* People who look at the past this way aren't really looking for answers. They're looking for gratification. I mean, Calgary is always trying to remake itself. It's always trying to be something other than it used to be, and to pull this off the past can't really exist. Even when it's got a past, it's a fabricated past. Reinterpreted. So, it's an uphill battle. But if I can get somebody to remember one thing that helps establish in their mind that, yes, they're part of a continuum, this isn't all there is, there's a future and there was a past, even if it's somebody driving past that corner and saying, 'Oh yah, I read a story about the building that used to be there and it was a funny story.' Even that puts a time line in someone's mind."

Harry and I walk east across the rails of the Light Rail Transit line that the elderly ladies of Sunnyside could not stop, the train's bell clanging in warning even after its cars have slipped quietly past us. Our path takes us through the original town site that took shape in the 1880s, a triangle of roughly twenty-two thousand acres of flatland in the bend of the Bow River, bordered in the south by the CPR line. Today this area is mostly downtown high-rise development, office and residential towers with a scattering of leftover homes and businesses for which developers have not yet managed to imagine replacements. The city blocks between the train tracks and the river are identically sized squares, so if you were to view the area from above it would resemble a pyramid about sixteen blocks wide at its southern base along the rail line, tapering toward its peak at the riverside, about nine blocks north of the tracks. On a hundred-year-old Dominion Lands Office survey map there is no settlement worthy of being marked here—only the tracks, two cart trails, one south and one north of the river, along with about fifty irregularly shaped parcels of land that had been staked out by homesteaders.

Harry tells me that the myth of Calgary as a colourful, fun-loving, Wild West town was already taking shape about a century ago.

"Think of the Stampede," he says, "as the beginning of a kind of revisionism in Calgary. The Stampede is a perfect example of how this city has always created its own false history. By the 1890s, the day of the big rancher was over. In 1896, Laurier's government got in. They were the farmers' party, and the Conservatives were the ranchers' party. The Liberals were hell-bent on throwing open the big leases to let the homesteaders come in. Ranching was already dying as a way of life, and the Stampede was a way of trying to recapture that, sort of like Wild Bill's Wild West Show. I mean, it was already over by the time they started the show. A friend of mine who did work on the labour history of Calgary insists that we've inherited a strong strain of revisionism when it comes to this city's past—this story of how this was a Wild West town, fun-loving, full of colourful people and everybody having a good time. He says that even as early as the teens, Calgarians were talking about the old days and glorifying this Wild West past. Calgary is what it chooses to be in every generation. The Stampede is just one of the first examples of the way it forgets what it used to be."

Harry tells me that his mother's family lived in Victoria Park, a neighbourhood on the east side of downtown, near to what is now the Stampede grounds. This area too housed its share of hard-up early Jewish

Calgarians. Today it is completely picked apart, like an unfinished jigsaw puzzle of tumbledown buildings, parking lots, warehouses and fuzzy grassed-over islands, where tomcats and gophers try to get themselves down low in the cooler undergrowth.

"It's a neighbourhood that has almost completely disappeared," Harry tells me. "There are almost no old buildings left. I was a census taker there a few years ago. The city was glad someone would volunteer to take the census there because the area had a reputation for being rough. A lot of buildings were hovels, illegally divided, and flophouses where I couldn't find the manager, and nobody could accurately say how many people lived in the building or even how many living units there were. A lot of the people I met were not too inviting to a census taker. My thought was don't these people know that the city builds roads for them and sewers and schools? But my sister said these are the people who are totally ignored and they're not going to benefit from the census and they don't care about you."

It is this community of the dispossessed and the elderly, and those who can afford only the lowest downtown rents, who make areas like Victoria Park home. Neighbourhoods like this are weird interregnums—limbolands—not yet a part of the new city, though their old routines and relationships with the rest of Calgary have been destroyed. Soon enough they too disappear.

As Harry and I talk, we walk along the first-developed streets of Calgary. We pass half unmade, half remade blocks: parking lots beside open fields in the shadow of green and pastel postmodernish head offices that went up toward the end of the last boom, when the downtown was supposed to keep sprawling westward along the river's edge. A few original frame houses and bungalows survive, with front porch doors swinging open and old rusted Studebakers and Volkswagen vans parked out back in plank board garages. These remind me of the garage that stood at the back of my grandfather's yard. Inside, it smelled of ancient oiled dirt, and there was a cast-iron pot belly stove against one wall with a tin chimney that reached up to the ceiling.

*Still life with Studebaker,
in the back alley behind
Ravvin's Furniture*

Nobody could help but notice that the area where Kerr had built his mill is undergoing a kind of renaissance. The Eau Claire public market and riverside condominiums have replaced what was an odd mix of warehouses, dilapidated homes and strip clubs. The city has run an impressive bike path along the river bank, which connects with a bridge crossing to the large urban park called Prince's Island.

Harry rather conspicuously ignores all this new development, giving it neither his criticism nor his compliment. Instead, he explains his deeper feelings about Calgary's recent economic turnaround and the latest version of itself that a boosterish city government is promoting.

"When I worked at City Hall near Olympic Plaza, it was very popular among people who worked downtown. To them it symbolized the success of the Winter Olympics, and everyone was saying, 'Finally there's a place to go! There's something here!' To me that plaza is nothing.

There's nothing there. There used to be something there. There were little shops, there were merchants, there were second-hand stores. They were interesting."

As if out of a dream, we're interrupted by a rough old character with a yellow beard, greasy blue baseball hat, a belly like a barrel pressing above his belt under a worn T-shirt.

"Can you tell me," he asks in a polite voice, almost too quiet to be heard above the traffic, "the way to the Alexandra Hotel?"

I draw a blank, but Harry explains that the Alexandra was torn down years ago. The news causes the old fellow to lose his words. Tears appear in his eyes and he bites his lip, nodding at us ever so slightly. Where, he must have wondered, would he go instead? And where, I wondered, had he been the last ten or fifteen years? This was one of the men of an older Calgary, an obsolete figure. The old-fashioned pride I imagine he had in his circle of drinking buddies was a bit like my grandfather's pride in the fact that his house on Seventh Avenue was built by a doctor. What a leap of the imagination! A grocer, Russian-born, who sold potatoes and cigarettes till midnight in his confectionery, owned something that had been built by a doctor.

After Harry and I part, I cut across the empty lots opposite the Sunset Billiards, then cross Eleventh Street and turn the corner. The site of my grandfather's prized house sits in the late afternoon light. There's the ever-present Calgary dust, but the air is hot and dry as it would have been in the city's youth. The last boom and bust cycle has reduced the property to a new kind of frontier: bald parking lot instead of prairie, treeless, awaiting development. There are a few leftover houses nearby, built by working men in the twenties, a few short blocks from the riverside. This strange precinct is one of the city's limbolands—a neighbourhood lost in time like Harry Sanders' Victoria Park. And while it is in limbo, I wonder, who keeps the time on these streets, where long ago, my grandfather's carefully wound clock kept perfect Calgary time. Where my dad put in his hours behind the counter at the grocery store, doing his homework between customers, while my grandfather trimmed his shrubs. Where Dr. Burgess Quint, the man who built the house, dressed like a Victorian dandy wearing a three-button felt jacket, a starched collar tickling his grey beard, a foulard the colour of oranges held in place at his throat by a ruby stick pin, would stroll by, amused as always, to see the man who bought his house scraping away in the soil.

Very little remains of the first generation of Calgary's buildings, which were built by and lived in by men like my grandfather. One of the oldest surviving structures is a wooden house that sits near the new Eau Claire market, a few hundred yards from the river. Like so many historic buildings in Calgary, it has been converted into a restaurant called the 1886 Café. Its pressed-tin roof and wide maple-floor planking are apparently original fixtures from the office of Kerr's lumber concern, which began operating the year the café takes for its name.

The place is busy on a Saturday morning, with youngish locals and a few tourists there for a break from hotel food. Four stuffed buffalo heads hang on the walls alongside shelves filled with carved horses, framed photos and clocks. Clocks are the key collectible here. Oddly enough, there is a token of my father's buried Calgary at the 1886 Café. On the south wall is the clock that hung on my grandfather's wall at 1116 – 7th Avenue. After my grandfather moved out of his house, the clock was moved to our house, only to be sold ignominiously at a garage sale after my father died. Presently, and most likely for good, the clock has stopped. When I was a child, watching its innards at work on our family room wall, I would never have guessed it would return to the streets where it had originally hung, to be looked at blankly by tourists and the bulging eyes of stuffed buffalo.

Border Crossings in
Hidden Canada

A decade before the outbreak of the American Civil War, a Delaware-born woman named Mary Shadd published a rather unusual guide for prospective U.S. immigrants to Canada. At the same time that Catharine Parr Traill and Susanna Moodie were informing British settlers about the joys and hardships of the Ontario bush, Shadd wrote her guide for the free blacks of the American north, whose liberty was newly threatened by the Fugitive Slave Act of 1850. This law entitled slave owners to hunt down escaped slaves in any American jurisdiction. Shadd's *A Plea for Emigration; Or, Notes of Canada West* drew a careful portrait of the "thirty thousand colored freemen of Canada," holding them up as an example of black well-being and accomplishment.

A recent edition of Shadd's *A Plea for Emigration* is the guide's first appearance in print since it was brought out by a Detroit print jobber in 1852, full of typos, at the price of twelve and a half cents a copy. The new edition of *A Plea* recovers for Canadian readers the history of an important suffragette. Shadd was one of the first women to travel on the Canadian lecture circuit. She edited, under a male pseudonym, an influential abolitionist newspaper, and in her later years, having returned to post–Civil War America, she agitated for women's right to vote. But if we read Shadd's guide with the Ontario landscape in mind, with an eye to discovering the broader historical currents that formed it, *A Plea* reveals a deeper, largely forgotten entanglement between black America and Canada.

Mary Shadd's childhood experiences taught her first-hand about the difference between a black life led in America and one led in Canada. She was the daughter of parents whose Delaware home was a stop on the Underground Railroad. These two words conjure images of rolling stock on subterranean tracks, but, quite simply, the Underground Railroad was made up of a network of abolitionists, Quakers and influential free blacks who shuttled escaped slaves from as far away as the Deep South to safe houses in the northern free states before spiriting them across the border to Canada. The "railroad" had stockholders who supported it financially; it had conductors who drove carts full of passengers or manned river-boats; it had stations that consisted of an abolitionist's home or a barn; and, of course, it had cargo—many thousands of people who found their way from Tennessee, Kentucky, Ohio and Pennsylvania.

In Canada, governments and social developments had made slavery as good as extinct. Following John Simcoe's anti-slavery act of 1793, rumour of Canada's openness to the idea of emancipation circulated freely in the southern States. And in 1833, slavery was abolished outright throughout the British Empire. This contrast put the Canada–U.S. border in a very particular light—in the midnineteenth century it symbolized two different ways of life, and, possibly, Canadian colour-blindness and sweet-spiritedness in the face of American racial strife.

In the midnineteenth century, Canada looked, to American blacks, like a unique society, with its law banning the introduction of slaves and the absence of an economic system based on agricultural plantations relying on unpaid labour. Shadd's guide to immigration was not written for the most desperate of American blacks who might cover a hundred miles of Ohio forest by night, following the North Star; it's the sort of book one can imagine free black families studying after dinner as they weighed their future in a slave-holding society.

In Shadd's view, the Fugitive Slave Act made life in America "dangerous in the extreme" for all blacks. In her view, back-to-Africa organizations, led by both well-meaning blacks and cynical whites, put the like-lihood of black assimilation in the U.S. under further threat. Shadd, who arrived in Toronto in 1856, tells her reader that rumours of Canada's frigid climate are overstated, but more importantly, that it is no fairy tale that the country offers blacks liberty in a way that American society never would. She wants her readers to consider the comfort with which she joined large white congregations in Toronto's churches. Her philosophy is one of self-reliance: "With an axe and a little energy," she argues, "an independent position" will be available to any newcomer. At times her enthusiasm for Canada is misleading. With an almost utopian fervor, she exclaims that in Canada, "no man's complexion" affects his business.

Most of what Canadians know about the history of black North Americans is viewed through the prism of events that took place in the United States: Civil War, Selma, the assassination of Martin Luther King, Jr., the fury of riots that destroyed the inner cities of Detroit and Newark, leaving abandoned blocks that still crumble as they stand. But whether we think about it or not, Canadians are intimately entangled with the heritage of black Americans. Particularly in southwestern Ontario, along a 180-mile stretch from Windsor to Brantford, black set-tlement has left an important mark on the landscape and local culture. The arrival of black settlers in the area is, in part, an American story—the story of tens of thousands of slaves who fled north in the first half of the nineteenth century. At no other time—aside from the flow of draft dodgers to Canada during the Vietnam War—have Americans sought a Canadian refuge with such near-religious fervor.

But the outcome of this influx, both the way it changed many Ontario communities and its low profile in our history books, is a purely Canadian tale, which I set out to learn by driving a route the tourism department of Ontario's short-lived NDP government dubbed the African–Canadian Heritage Tour. The route covers an area through the Detroit–Windsor corridor well into southwestern Ontario, and it repre-sents one of the first sustained efforts by the Ontario government to raise the profile of black history, as well as to encourage school teachers and tourists to recognize that history's crucial role in southern Ontario's collective identity. The sites that make up the tour focus on the period between 1815 and 1860, when fugitive slaves came to Canada in the greatest numbers. It was toward the end of this period, in 1850, that Mary Shadd settled in Windsor, a key point of entry for blacks fleeing the U.S.

While Mary Shadd's book reflects a unique aspect of black history at midcentury—an orderly immigration to Canadian centres of working and middle class blacks who hoped to assimilate into mainstream society—the African–Canadian Heritage Tour reflects a somewhat different, more embittered history: the flight of escaped slaves into the unknown North. Still, as I visited the churches, museums and restored safe houses that mark the Heritage Tour, it became clear that Mary Shadd's legacy haunts much of the region's history.

To join the African–Canadian Heritage Tour from Toronto you travel first along the lake front and through the city's western suburbs, one of the most historyless routes imaginable. Its landmarks are massive billboard ads for Inglis, Mazda, JVC, Toyota and Fuji, which shimmer in the heat by day and pulsate a neon red by night. One particularly distracting ad for American Airlines flashes a hundred different destinations with the present cost to fly—Orlando $495; Kalamazoo $600. Heading west out of the city, there are a few relics of old Toronto visible from the Expressway: Fort York, used by the British to repel an American invading force; the white plaster-winged Victory that crowns the entrance gate to the Exhibition Grounds; the Palais Royal, a war-era dance hall along the lake front, next to a red brick Legion Hall sitting high above the water.

As the city falls away behind my car, I see a high wall of noise guards separating the roadway from suburban neighbourhood streets; the sky a kind of hazy blue-grey, a murky pillow of sky that doesn't so much cover you as press down on the countryside. Soon come Mississauga, Streetsville, then Halton Hills (real estate fortunes and milk are made there). The people who settled this landscape, who broke it up into farms and mill yards, named their towns to commemorate faraway history—important accomplishments at Cambridge and Waterloo—not after the important events of the immediate environs. This tendency to think of history as something that happened long ago in Europe may play a part in the relatively low profile of the history of black American settlement in Ontario.

Each stop along the African–Canadian Heritage Tour marks a site where fugitive blacks settled. The bulk of these are not far across the Michigan border, in a northeasterly line above the Canadian shore of Lake Erie. The most famous black American-turned-Canadian of the nineteenth century is Josiah Henson, a Methodist preacher and entrepreneur who, in 1830, arrived in the area where the town of Dresden is located today. Henson's Dawn settlement, twenty miles east of the American border, predated the founding of Dresden by thirteen years, and his establishment of a vocational school for fugitive slaves, as well as the beginnings of a self-sufficient black colony, make him one of the area's early pioneers.

Mary Shadd had grave doubts about the kind of exclusive community Henson built. Anything that smacked to her of segregationist ideals seemed to replicate the black experience of disenfranchisement in America. To her mind, the tendency among Canadian blacks to join all-black churches or to accept government funding of special black schools would only help guarantee an isolated future for their children. In the same way, she approved of Henson's Dawn settlement as long as it did not "exclude whites from [its] vicinity."

At Dresden today, Henson's great-great-granddaughter, Barbara Carter, is the director of an impressive interpretation centre and museum dedicated to the memory of Henson's escape from slavery and his accomplishments in founding the Dawn cooperative settlement. I met Carter in one of the museum's restored buildings, a 140-year-old pioneer church that contains the organ and pulpit from the sanctuary where Henson preached. Though the building has the spic-and-span neatness of a restored antique, its square nails and rough walnut siding recall the appearance it would have had when Henson's followers were first clearing the land.

The first thing Carter and I had to sort out was why her museum has two seemingly interchangeable names: The Reverend Josiah Henson House and Uncle Tom's Cabin Historic Site. It's commonly thought that Henson's life formed the basis for Harriet Beecher Stowe's famous anti-slavery book, *Uncle Tom's Cabin,* though there's no hard proof that Barbara Carter's great-great-grandfather ever met the author. In Stowe's novel, Uncle Tom is a kind-hearted Christian slave who falls into the hands of a cruel planter and is beaten to death when he refuses to reveal the whereabouts of two escaped slaves. The life of Carter's great-great-grandfather is obscured, not only by Stowe's fictional portrait, but by the numerous ghost-written editions of Henson's autobiography. *The Life of Josiah Henson: Formerly a Slave,* first published in 1849 in Boston, became a favourite among Victorian readers, but the details in it tended to change as the narrative went though repeated editions. One aspect of Henson's *Life* that remains constant, however, is his familiar fugitive's story of flight, which begins with travels north by night through Indian country to Cincinnati. From there Henson continues on foot through Ohio, all the time avoiding "Kentucky spies" who might be on the lookout for escaped slaves. Finally, friendly boatmen take him and his family from Buffalo to the Canadian shore in exchange for work.

Carter acknowledges that it has been difficult serving the Canadian historical record about Henson's life when a fictional record by a rather melodramatic American writer holds the public's attention. Many of the details of her great-great-grandfather's experience are forgotten in the shadow of Stowe's fictional account, in particular his accomplishments at Dawn.

"But we have a lot of documentation," she says. "We know from Mrs. Stowe's own words that Josiah Henson was the man she had in mind when she created her Uncle Tom."

It's clear that Carter finds herself in a bit of a bind when deciding how to tell Henson's story. She'd like to strip it of the myth and melo-drama, but doesn't want to completely jettison the notoriety that attach-es to Henson through his relationship with Stowe's novel.

"When Josiah Henson arrived here," Carter tells me, "this was virgin ground. We can hardly imagine because we have none of the forest around us. He helped establish the British American Institute, a vocational school and, with the support of New York Quakers, land was bought for black settlers to farm. At its height Dawn boasted five hundred inhabitants. Fifteen hundred acres were planted with tobacco, corn and oats. A small mill went into production, processing the wood felled in the surrounding walnut forests. Henson took some of the walnut board the mill produced to London when he visited the Crystal Place and Windsor Castle to meet with Queen Victoria."

It's difficult to imagine the Dresden area as a wood lot supporting a saw and grist mill. Today the flat land on the banks of the Sydenham River is as domesticated as any farm country in Canada. There are a few lone stands of walnut trees down the road toward Chatham, but trees are sparse, left standing in spots to mark the edges of property. A hard wind blows ceaselessly across the surrounding sections of unprotected cropland.

Carter's industrious commitment to her museum helped secure a $1.2 million grant from Ontario's NDP government. The museum has a modern, high-tech feel, and visitors move from gift and book stores to exhibition rooms to the well-preserved buildings gathered in a fenced yard behind the centre. But the question of who Carter's great-great-grandfather was, and where his story fits into black Canadian history, is not simple to answer. The increasing association between Henson and Stowe's Uncle Tom has distracted people from Henson's Canadian accomplishments, turning him, rather strangely, from a Canadian pioneer and visionary, who encouraged vocational skills and economic independence among his followers, into a moralizing fictional character in an American novel. Historians question whether Stowe had heard of Henson when she was writing her book and suggest that she may have latched onto his story later, relying on the narrative she read in his autobiography as proof that she was a reliable informant on slave matters. Even Carter admits, when pressed, that Stowe's interest in slavery was not necessarily founded on purely humanitarian concerns.

"I wish she'd been more accurate about slavery," Carter tells me. "She had no great love of my great-great-grandfather. She wanted to sell books."

Carter is quick to point to the problems that arise when stories like Josiah Henson's are sensationalized for the pleasure of white audiences rather than for any educational purposes.

"The sentimentalization began with Stowe," Carter says. "And her book was very influential. Well into the 1930s, *Uncle Tom's Cabin* was the most commonly taught text in Canadian secondary schools. But she could hardly be blamed for the cringing, demeaning versions of her characters who began showing up in vaudeville and burlesque shows. Travelling troupes presented a distorted version of her characters to huge audiences for nearly eighty years. Called Tom Shows, these had nothing to do with the history of fugitives. It was just black face—stuff that white audiences gobbled up."

Ironically, American travelling shows of this kind passed through Dresden in 1919 and 1923, a mile or so from where Josiah Henson had made his greatest impact.

"We talked at great length on whether the name Uncle Tom ought to be attached to this site," Carter admits. "And we decided that it's very hard to change something where people aren't schooled accurately in history. I'll give you an example of the quandary we're in. At the corner where you turn to come down to the site, we have a sign that says, 'Josiah Henson House.' You would be amazed at how many people are upset because that doesn't say, 'Uncle Tom's Cabin.' They don't want to see Josiah Henson. They want to see Uncle Tom's cabin." (In my Rand McNally road atlas of Canada and the United States the site is marked as "Uncle Tom's Cabin Museum.")

Out back of the interpretation centre, a rather fresh-looking, two-storey house billed as Uncle Tom's Cabin is set among other relics of the Dawn fugitive slave community: a trim wooden church, another high-peaked, refurbished settler's cottage and a hollowed out tree trunk, five feet wide, which was used as a smoke house for curing meat. At the edge of the interpretive centre's grounds, the tombstones of the com-

Gravestones of fugitive slaves who settled near the site of Josiah Henson's house

munity's first inhabitants have been gathered and embedded in a cement wall by the roadside. Nearby is Henson's own gravestone, an impressive white marker with masonic symbols on its face, topped with a distinctly imperial-looking, granite crown.

When I ask Carter which of the relics gathered about the grounds is most dear to her, she mentions the family graveyard.

"It's the one thing that still connects us with community," she explains.

Beyond these objects nothing remains of the Dawn settlement that Henson founded. And the once substantial black population around Dresden has dwindled.

"Young people go to the cities," Carter says. "When I was a young girl, sixteen years old, the population was twenty-five hundred people. Thirty, forty years later it's not much more than that. There's no great industry to hold our young people."

North Buxton, a tiny blink-of-an-eye place twenty miles south of Dresden, bills itself as one of the only pre–Civil War black settlements in

Canada still in existence. The town site is twenty minutes by car from the Lake Erie Shore, and the township roads leading into North Buxton run alongside fields of wheat, corn and soybeans. In its heyday black-owned farms ran all the way from the town to the lake. Nowadays, black families still own farms and businesses in the area, but the most notable markers of black life are the Centennial Museum and the old schoolhouse, which is itself a museum. The local school board brings kids from the surrounding towns to hear how fugitive slaves populated what was originally forest.

The North Buxton Centennial Museum has none of the flash and sparkle of Barbara Carter's interpretation centre. A low-slung building funded with federal money at the time of Expo '67, it houses a haphazard collection of artifacts and photographs. They manage to convey the texture of the homesteading life fugitives led more effectively than a new, more polished exhibition can. There's the usual potpourri of estate leftovers: buttons, irons, canes, Bibles, eyeglasses and family photographs. The museum's dusky interior approximates the overstuffed living room of a prosperous, turn-of-the-century, North Buxton citizen. Included in the collection are the Shadd family papers, among which is a ledger that belonged to Mary Shadd's father, listing every pair of shoes he sold to customers from Delaware to Canada. The museum also holds the subscription receipts for the *Provincial Freeman,* the abolitionist newspaper Shadd edited.

"We have the original Josiah Henson," I'm told by Alice Newby, who curates the Buxton Centennial Museum. At first I think Newby is talking about some bit of pickled remains in a jar, but she points at a photo of a familiar, full-bearded face that hangs in the late afternoon half-light.

"That was the original," she tells me. "It hung in his house. He was married twice. He left things to his wife, and their kids intermarried with people here. And that's how the photo came to Buxton. Dawn's gone," Newby explains as she leads me into her sunlit, book-and-paper-cluttered office at the back of the museum. "I'm forty-one years old. There hasn't been anything there since I've been alive. You go down the base-line road and at one time that was all black farms. Now 90 per cent of that's gone."

Newby's pleasure at having the "original" Josiah Henson is understandable. The portrait offers indisputable contact with the early days of the area's black settlements, when fugitive slaves came up from safe houses along the Underground Railroad in Delaware and Pennsylvania. But Newby doesn't think of North Buxton or any of the Canadian sites on the African–Canadian Heritage Tour as "terminals" on the Underground Railroad.

"When people refer to places like Buxton," Newby continues, "as the northernmost terminus on the Underground Railroad, I say, 'Once you'd crossed the Detroit River, once you'd come across the water, you were free. This was a haven for escaped slaves. Slaves came here and made a life for themselves.

"King chose the land because of access to Lake Erie," Newby explains, referring to the white abolitionist Reverend William King, who was largely responsible for enticing fugitive slaves to settle near Buxton. "The land was given to the settlers at the settlements at Collingwood and Sandwich. But here they had to buy their land. Houses had to be a certain size—at least eighteen by twenty feet. And King didn't press vocational education at the school the way they did at Dawn. The school at North Buxton gained a reputation for being the best in the area. King wanted the classics taught. Eventually, you had American blacks coming up here because they'd heard of the school. There were sawmills here. They had a brickyard. And there was a hotel. But without King it wouldn't have happened. I think he wanted to prove something to people in the States. He wanted to prove that blacks could be self-sufficient and independent."

Newby's family—prosperous, educated people who helped slaves escape from the States—came to the North Buxton area in the mid-nineteenth century and settled on the outskirts of what was then called the Elgin settlement. Like Henson's Dawn, Elgin was a refuge for fleeing slaves, where they could join a cooperative and economically viable black community. Elgin lasted longer and was more successful than Henson's Dawn. King raised money through his Presbyterian contacts, from prominent blacks and from forward-looking philanthropists in Toronto and Montréal. By the 1850s, when Shadd was writing, the settlement consisted of nearly nine thousand acres. But again, it was the community's exclusivity that led her to reject its principles. Since it was only willing to sell land to fugitive slaves, Shadd felt it discriminated against free American blacks who had been put in danger by the Fugitive Slave Act.

Many of the people who settled near Buxton went back to the United States once the North won the Civil War, just as Shadd did.

"If you look at census records," Newby explains, "you'd see that a lot of the fugitives who came up had left family behind. So after the Civil War, they went back. It didn't necessarily have to be wives and children. Some went back to find their parents. They felt that they should take their talents—the education they'd acquired here—back home to help with reconstruction."

This southward exodus has made North Buxton more a focus of pride and interest among Americans than among black Canadians. Newby explains, "There's lots of families in the States who know one thing: that their people came to Canada. And the objects and documents in this museum, along with the church and the schoolhouse, are very important to them. These were built by people who were slaves. You know, hammering the nails. People on tours will walk up to the church wall and touch it. They can barely believe it was built by runaway slaves. I had one woman tell me she couldn't believe she was walking where runaway slaves had walked."

Though slavery and the Underground Railroad are American phenomena, there has been a relative absence of historical markers in the U.S. connecting people to the paths taken by fugitive slaves to freedom.

"We know how the Underground Railroad worked down there," Newby says. "Where they would cross and who helped the fugitives. We know because we have letters and other documents. But think about it: everything on American ground had to be hidden. So we can say, 'This

An early black settler's
house near Buxton

might have been a station on the Underground Railroad.' We can guess what trap doors and hidden rooms were used for. But it's in Canada, in places like North Buxton, where we've got the actual artifacts. The physical stuff that conjures up what those people went through."

As with Josiah Henson's story, it is people who live south of the border who have the biggest stake in preserving the memory of life at North Buxton. So they come to Canada in an effort to learn about their ancestors' lives. As I let the screen door of Newby's museum swing shut behind me, I wonder if it is American or Canadian history I am tracking down. Or both. Across the road from Buxton's Centennial Museum is a farmhouse that was once owned by fugitive slaves. It's boarded and ready, I'm told, to be dragged off somewhere by the farmer who owns the land it stands on. A little way up the road, women are setting up a flea market in a farmyard; a tribe of grey-feathered hens keeps an eye on things. "Worms $1," says a sign posted along the roadside. These things could be anywhere at all in rural Canada. Or rural America for that matter.

As I travel the African–Canadian Heritage Tour between Toronto and Windsor, driving up and down the township roads between the Erie beaches and the flat farm lands around Dresden, my conversations with people often circle back to the way mainstream Canadians of the last century dealt with growing numbers of black citizens in southwestern Ontario towns.

In Chatham, a small city on the banks of the Thames River, south of Dresden and a few miles nearer to Windsor, I talk with people at the First Baptist Church whose earliest founders were deeply committed to the anti-slavery movement and the Underground Railroad. Virginia Travis, the church's archivist and historian ushers me into a wood-panelled sitting room where we are joined by one of the community's elders, a woman who introduces herself, rather warily, as Ruby. The room is filled with a buttery afternoon light that falls through glazed windows. We are surrounded by shelves packed with mementoes from the church's years of involvement in what Virginia Travis calls the country's first freedom movement. Among these, she points out a table and chair said to have been used by anti-slavery crusader John Brown on one of his secretive visits to Chatham.

"Brown's idea," Travis says, "was to get a band together—a band of warriors—who could aid him in his plans to attack the U.S. arsenal at Harpers Ferry, Virginia. He hoped to touch off a nationwide struggle that would end slavery for good. Brown came here in the 1850s because he saw the possibility of the support offered by well-educated people. At the time, the population of Chatham was somewhere between one-third and two-thirds black. He saw the community of freed ex-slaves that flourished here as a wonderful opportunity."

John Brown did find support in Chatham. Again, the American racial predicament was uppermost in the minds of black Canadians. The prominent Shadd family gave him support—a good number of them attending his secretive meetings—and the printer of the locally owned abolitionist paper became one of Brown's Chatham compatriots who actually travelled south and took part in a disastrous attack. But even when travelling miles into Canadian territory, Brown was careful to keep his visits secret, and nothing like a majority of Chatham's black population felt comfortable backing his radical plans.

"Not everyone wanted to admit they were a former slave," Travis explains. "Or who they were a slave to. In those days, bounty hunters came to the border. The Fugitive Slave law was in place, so when people came north they changed their names." This fear of being captured by slave catchers in Chatham justifies Mary Shadd's belief that the 1850 law made life precarious for every freed black, as well as escaped slaves.

In the mid-1850s the *Provincial Freeman* was published in Chatham, and though Shadd had moved to the area, she had given up the editorship after her decision to stop using a male pseudonym brought a rush of negative public reaction. While in Chatham she hosted John Brown and sat in on meetings of the Chatham Convention, which made secret plans to attack the Virginia Armory in the hope of inciting a slave rebellion. The attack was a failure, leading to Brown's execution, but it did hasten the Civil War, and Shadd helped one of Brown's compatriot's write a memoir of these events called *A Voice From Harpers Ferry*.

In so many of her endeavors, it was Shadd's skills as a journalist that made her voice memorable and powerful. In *A Plea* she consults almanacs for information on Canadian soil, includes a graph of average temperatures in winter and summer, provides the exchange rates between U.S. and Canadian currency, and excerpts liberally from the "Law of Succession in Upper Canada," which ensured black citizens' rights to pass on property to their next of kin.

As Travis and I talk about Brown's connections at Chatham, her companion looks me over with a questioning if not disparaging eye. *What's this white man want with this history?* Ruby seems to wonder. *And exactly what is it he's getting at by asking what it's like to be black in Chatham today?* Ruby listens as Virginia Travis answers my questions about John

Brown, but she sits up a little straighter as we begin to talk about recent events. Then she breaks into the conversation politely, without a hint of rancour in her voice.

"In the 1950s there was subtle racism here," she begins. "And there were places in Chatham where you were not wanted. But you knew that, so you didn't go there. I was taught not to go where I wasn't wanted. If I wanted an ice cream cone, I was not to spend my father's hard-earned money at a restaurant that wouldn't serve us if we wanted to sit down and eat. In my youth, the only job the black women could get was as a domestic, where you had to go in the back door or the side door. At the theatre you had to sit upstairs in the balcony. You couldn't get a job as a clerk at the department stores. You could work the elevator—I did that—but you couldn't get a job as a clerk on the floor. You really weren't welcome in the churches either. As recently as three years ago, the choir from the Detroit Second Baptist was here to sing at one of the white churches. Myself and a couple other girls planned to go, and we were supposed to meet, but we missed each other, so we just grabbed a seat and I ended up on the lower level. The other girls were up in the balcony. A white couple came in on the lower level, and they left in a hurry. They went upstairs and saw my friend and said, 'Well, they're up here too.' Right here in Chatham. Just a few years ago. If you got a place to live, it had to be in the East End. You had to be on Park Street or Wellington or King."

Ruby's anecdote about the church does away with any myth of Canada, the sweet and happily diverse. But there is something Canadian too in the polite, almost upbeat way she recalls a very real colour bar in the heart of central Canada. The African–Canadian Heritage Tour goes some distance toward making up for the fact that most Canadians have no idea that black Ontarians and their compatriots played a substantial role in events connected with slavery and the Civil War. A song most of us heard as kids goes as follows:

John Brown's body lies a-mouldering in the grave
But his truth goes marching on.

When I picked out the notes of this American standard on our family's piano, I assumed that its main character was some mythical figure, a larger-than-life American type like Johnny Appleseed or John Henry, that steel driving man. I couldn't have imagined I'd sit at a desk where Brown sat not long before a Virginian hangman—black-hooded to remain anonymous—meted out the punishment deemed suitable for American traitors who made secret plans with the free blacks of Canada.

The African–Canadian Heritage Tour winds its way along a corridor of southern Ontario that is really a peninsula bounded on the north by Lake St. Clair, in the south by the Erie shore and in the west by the Detroit River. The area is known for its wine producers and for the abundance of birds and butterflies that use the southern outcropping off Point Pelee as a migratory stopping place. As I travel west toward Windsor, I pass Maidstone township, where I run across one of the quirkier stops connected with the Underground Railroad. This is the John Freeman Walls Historic Site, which is a family-run operation located on Puce Road, a quick turn off the highway.

Here, like the road that runs from North Buxton down to the Erie shore, as many as seventy families descended from fugitive slaves once farmed and supported the activities of three churches. And here, like Barbara Carter's Josiah Henson House Museum, the site is overseen by the great-great-grandchild of a man who came to Canada—in this case from North Carolina—around the middle of the last century. I'd not written or called to let Bryan Walls know I would drop in to meet him. When I arrive at his museum site, there are a few cars in the lot. A small group is being led about the grounds from one tumbledown wood building to another, and there is the steady sound of someone hammering or chopping wood in the distance. The first man I meet, who offers to take me around the site, turns out to be Bahamian, a nephew of Walls who was studying at night at the University of Windsor while working by day as a tour guide. When I tell him my reason for visiting and that I would like to tape record what he describes as we tour the site, he decides to check with his uncle.

The John Freeman Walls Historic Site near Windsor

Bryan Walls' first response to me is polite but careful. He listens as I describe my interest in black Canadian history and says very little in response. I am another writer who wants to retell a story he feels is rightfully his to tell (he has published his own book on the history of his family's life in Essex County). Gradually, he drops his guard, showing me a video of a TV appearance he'd made on Pat Robertson's 700 Club. Then we walk outside and sit on a picnic bench near the log house where his great-great-grandfather and grandmother first homesteaded after they'd escaped to Canada.

Bryan Walls' commemorative museum has a strong religious impulse, and he is quick to insist that the Maidstone area and his ancestors' experience settling on the Puce Road offer proof of the possibilities of Canadian racial harmony.

"The whole area is like a microcosm of what the world should be like. My grandfather always said the people ate together, built barns together and kept love in their hearts for each other."

The source of most of Walls' family stories is his Aunt Stella, a woman he refers to as a *griot*, using the African term meaning "keeper of the oral history."

"According to Stella," Walls says, "once John Freeman Walls arrived in Canada he would never have considered returning to the United States, even after the Civil War. He felt he would have put himself in harm's way by doing that."

Walls views his forbears' flight to Canada and their decision to settle at the end of the Underground Railroad as an almost forgotten portion of American, Canadian and black history.

"It's like the unfolding of the tomb of Tutankhamen," he tells me, "in terms of historical wealth and significance. There's abandoned cemeteries all around here with inscriptions like: Henry Jackson, Born a slave in Kentucky, died a free man in Canada."

I ask Walls how blacks from large Canadian communities like Toronto view his museum.

"To tell you the truth," he says, "these places probably make them think, It's about time now. Eureka. I think they think of them as examples of courage, as symbols of our survival. These places are historical symbols of pride. And they give us confidence that finally our history's being considered important. Unless your history's considered important, you won't be considered important as a people. It's only now that we could do something like this. If we tried to do this in the 1930s, there would still have been a very good chance that we would have run into prejudice. But the feeling now is that this community has embraced what we're doing and encouraged us."

I can't help noticing as I get back into my car that my licence plate is in the minority in the parking lot, outnumbered by those from Michigan, Ohio, New York. I drive a little way down the Puce Road and pull over by the side of a farmer's field. I sit with my legs out the side of the car door, drinking coffee from a thermos cup as the trucks and cars roar by on Essex County's Route 25. Across the road a lush growth wavers in the wind—a crop I am unable to name—something big-leafed, green and low to the ground.

As I drive the last leg of the 401 into Windsor, I think about Bryan Walls' initial wary response to me. I consider his instinctive urge to protect his story from predators, from the type of writer who'd tell it badly. And then I consider the patient way I'd waited him out, not quite arguing with him, to convince him I wouldn't do that. I hadn't begged. I'd simply waited till he decided he'd take a chance. But I'm unsure of my own intentions. I wasn't very interested in a narrative of Canadian decency in the face of American crimes. If America was so brutal and Canada so sweet a haven, why did so many American blacks return, as Shadd did, when the Civil War was over?

To complete my travels on the African–Canadian Heritage Tour, I drive the most southerly leg of the 401 into Windsor, through the city's centre and into downtown Detroit through the Peace Tunnel. When I emerge on Jefferson Avenue, it is early evening, and crowds are gathering at the arena for a game. The big buildings cluster down by the shore, and in a matter of a few blocks, as I head up Woodward Avenue, I find myself surrounded on both sides by burned-out ruins—the aftermath, you might say, of slavery, as race war really did break out on the streets of Detroit in July 1967, ignited by white policemen raiding a black after-hours club. Five days of rioting, fire-setting and looting followed, destroying the heart of the city. I pass boarded factories and warehouses, blocks of businesses abandoned three decades ago, with hand-painted signs, wrought iron grates pulled down over shop windows, the odd front door broken open to reveal a showroom stuffed full of trash, mountains of newspaper and food tins and discarded plumbing fixtures. Traffic runs up and down Woodward as if this spectacle is nothing out of the ordinary. There are a few outposts of surviving commerce—a liquor store that accepts food stamps, bars with small groups of customers standing out front on the sidewalk, drinking beer out of plastic cups. Not far from here, at the corner of Gratiot Street and Woodward, there was an Underground Railroad station, where fugitive slaves hid before they made the last leg of their journey across the Detroit River to Windsor or nearby Amherstburg. And the printer of the first edition of Shadd's guide to black emigra-

The desolation of Detroit off Woodward Avenue, a long boulevard of broken dreams that leads to the pricey precincts of the city's outlying suburbs

tion—reputedly a Quaker who wanted to further her project of black emancipation—had his office not far from here.

Farther along Woodward the big old sandstone churches are in good shape, as is a giant temple with neoclassical pillars, once a synagogue, now an evangelical meeting house. This careful upkeep of structures devoted to an otherworldly home is unsettling in a neighbourhood where the things of this world are so utterly ruined. Surrounded by demolished buildings, a once-elegant apartment block of eight or nine stories stands empty, abandoned and worth less than nothing. No tourist in his or her right mind would come to see it, even though it is every bit as intricately designed, as miraculous in its continued existence as other famous ruins at Giza and Angkor Wat. This shell of an apartment block is an American house of the dead that every Canadian should see to understand the gap between our culture and that of our southern neighbours.

Back on the Canadian side of the Detroit River, in Amherstburg, I stop to look across the water at the American shore. What you see as you look from this small, well-preserved town toward the west is not the Detroit skyline, but a tear-shaped island called Bois Blanc, which sits in the middle of the river. Bois Blanc—or Boblo as the Americans call it—was named by the French when they came upon it in 1609 for its stand of white birch.

The island, a short boat ride from both American and Canadian coasts, falls under Canadian jurisdiction. In the 1920s and '30s, Bois Blanc was developed to serve as Detroit's version of Coney Island, with crowds of people ferrying across to picnic and play on its amusement rides. When the amusement business went into decline in the 1980s, investors dumped money into the island's fun park to no effect. Its latest incarnation has been engineered by Michigan businessman John Oram, who managed to buy the property for what seems to be a steal: $2.5 million. On it he is building a resort condominium community that will include a golf course, marinas and town-house developments with names like The Gold Coast and White Wood Ridge. Lots begin at U.S. ninety thousand and run as high as two hundred thousand.

The notable thing about all this is that John Oram's dream of creating a privately owned enclave will create a fortress for wealthy Americans out of a piece of land that once represented the first moment of Canadian freedom to America's most hunted inhabitants. In their flight from the South, along the secretive routes of the Underground Railroad, escaped slaves reached the narrowest points along the Detroit River, where boats were hired to take them across to the Canadian side. Many fugitive slaves found one ride to the west side of Bois Blanc and then arranged the final leg of their journey from the east side of the island to the British fort on the Canadian shore at Amherstburg.

You can't get across to see Bois Blanc Island these days unless you've got at least ninety thousand dollars handy. The only people using the ferry dock on this grey afternoon are construction workers, whose big dump trucks idle on the pavement as they wait to ride over and pick up another load of island dirt. When I walk out to the end of the ferry dock, getting my camera ready for a few shots, a woman comes rushing out of a sales office at the edge of the dock and calls down from a balcony to tell me I cannot shoot pictures of the island's green shoreline.

"That's private property," she says, trying not to sound too churlish as she points across the water. "And this is too." She indicates the ground where I stand. "Why don't you go talk to them back over there in the management office," she suggests. "They may be able to okay you."

"Sounds fair," I say as I march obediently from the pier and up to the little wood bungalow whose sign reads, "Bois Blanc Island Resort Community—Welcome to Boblo Island Today!"

The people inside the management office are not at all interested in letting me take photographs of their private preserve, even when I tell them I will just go up the shoreline to the Navy Yard Park in the centre of Amherstburg and take shots from there.

"Why don't you just do that then?" a woman behind the desk asks. Then she grabs a chirping telephone and sweetly speaks the resort's name into it.

Would it be cynical to say that there is something distinctly Canadian in the readiness with which an American businessman is sold a tract of land like Bois Blanc—a true landmark in the anti-slavery crusade? The sale is somehow an affront to the memory of the people who used the island as a stop in their flight to northern freedom, since Bois Blanc is a kind of gateway. It is the midpoint between the burned out ruins of those Detroit streets and the lush farm land of towns like Amherstburg, Windsor, Buxton, Dresden and Chatham.

A century and a half ago, the two sides of the Detroit River held distinctly different possibilities that no American or Canadian could overlook. But today, how central is our legacy—the legacy of tens of thousands of fugitive slaves who found a haven in towns like Sandwich, Colchester, Collingwood, Chatham, Buxton and Dresden? Did these events create a consciousness in Canada of its black citizens that includes an awareness of the meaning Canada held for their ancestors? The reappearance of Mary Shadd's *A Plea* gives us an opportunity to recover some sense of this history, some reason to look past a bulldozer's work on Bois Blanc and reclaim another, older story.

The Ghosts of Hirsch

The ghost towns in Hollywood movies—Rocky Mountain mining outposts gone dry or rodeo towns destroyed by an apocalyptic shoot-out—tend to retain their main-street architecture, a bit busted, good and dusty, but still standing long after the people have vanished. Ghost town sites on the Canadian prairie don't look nearly so romantic as their Hollywood counterparts. Abandoned prairie buildings, built solely of wood, were easily towed away and made use of at a new site, while buildings no one wanted any longer were torn down for their lumber or simply gave in to the unpredictability of weather and fire. As communities steadily shrink in the more isolated parts of the Canadian West, the landmarks of rural life—grain elevators, churches and schools—are taken apart and trucked away, leaving nothing but the footprints of vanished frames.

This slow remaking of the prairie landscape has been going on for more than a century. European farming practices obliterated native systems of land use, and the substantial decline of many agricultural communities, especially since the Second World War, has led to another unpeopling of the countryside, in many cases a reversion to wilderness. Relics of another era—like the round barn designed to shed snow, storefront saloons, wooden onion-domed churches built by Ukrainian farmers, barnside ads for Stanislaus Flour and Chinook Beer—stand as rare monuments to real ghost towns, which are as invisible as anything long dead.

A true ghost town is nothing more than an absence through which to watch the rolling grassland, marked here by fenceposts, there by the edge of a cleared forest, and now and again by the freak presence of an abandoned cemetery.

The Souris River Valley of southern Saskatchewan has its share of such ghostly places, many of them built and then abandoned by the unlikeliest of settlers. One of these vanished town sites is still called Hirsch on the map—though no one actually lives there any longer. From the 1880s until the Second World War, ten thousand difficult acres were put under cultivation by the Hirsch colony of forty families—one hundred and fifty souls at most—all of them Jewish immigrants from Russia and eastern Europe. The appearance of Jewish farmers on the Canadian prairies in the 1880s and '90s was an early chapter in the great flight of the poor and persecuted from eastern Europe, a social upheaval that coincided with efforts by the new Canadian government to settle its western lands and thwart American expansionism. Other Europeans—mostly Mennonites with centuries of farming in their blood—had already arrived on the prairies, escaping the severe political and religious persecutions of Czarist Russia. But the Jewish settlers were a different breed. The majority of farmers, who broke land at the Saskatchewan colonies located at Hirsch, Edenbridge, Hoffer, Wapella, Lipton and Qu'Apelle, came not from a farming tradition but from eastern Europe's landless urban class. Many were tradesmen and shopkeepers fleeing the Czarist pogroms and the hardships of the Russian army.

For Jews in Czarist Russia, the 1890s were not unlike the 1990s for the Albanians under Serbian rule in Kosovo. Pogroms, supported by Russian officials, led to widespread rape, looting and murder. The Czarist "May Laws" had expelled Jews from many hamlets and villages, and prohibited the sale or renting of land to them for agricultural purposes. Homes, businesses and farms were taken out of Jewish hands. Schools and synagogues were destroyed, and an unpredictable exodus of thousands began to flee west across the Russian border.

As Jews left Russia in large numbers, they often found themselves in a Canadian port—Halifax, Québec or Montréal—with the intention of travelling on to the United States. By 1891, it was becoming more difficult to enter America, and the Montréal Jewish community, which received the bulk of these new immigrants, found itself both unprepared and unwilling to absorb them all. The idea of moving large numbers of newcomers west to farm had been raised with the Federal government and was supported by the offer of 160 acres of fertile but rocky field in exchange for ten dollars, under Sir John A. Macdonald's North-West Territories settlement policy. The plan to move Jewish settlers to prairie colonies became a practical possibility when it gained the support of the German–Jewish financier Baron Maurice de Hirsch. In 1891, Hirsch, who had made his fortune developing the Oriental Railway linking Constantinople and Europe, created the Jewish Colonization Society (JCA), which took on the responsibility of transporting the new settlers and aiding them in establishing themselves as farmers. The JCA also supported Jewish farming colonies in New Jersey, Oregon, South Dakota, British Palestine, Brazil and Argentina, where a few colonies started by Jewish gauchos still exist. Described in the 1929 edition of the *Encyclopaedia Britannica* as "probably the greatest charitable trust in the world," the JCA channelled funds through its Montréal office to support the Canadian settlements and lobby the Canadian government to allow greater numbers of Jewish families to go west.

Baron de Hirsch's charitable work was, for its day, markedly modern and secular in nature. He gave his support to educational and vocational training centres in Europe, and his lack of faith in Zionism as the solution to Jewish homelessness led to a strong focus on resettling Russian, Polish and Romanian Jews in North and South America. In Galicia he funded the agricultural college of Slobodka Lesna, where students, many of whom had never seen a farm before, spent half their day in class and the other half working the land.

"My efforts shall show that the Jews have not lost the agricultural qualities that their forefathers possessed," wrote the baron in 1891. "I shall try to make for them a new home in different lands, where as free farmers on their own soil, they can make themselves useful to that country."

The JCA hired local land managers to choose a site for its first Canadian colony, and though they recognized the superiority of the farm land available near Regina, they chose a location in the far southeastern corner of Saskatchewan, since a few Jewish families had already landed there as farmers and shopkeepers serving the Canadian Pacific Railway (CPR) branch line. By this rather unpredictable route, Hirsch was established as a Jewish farming colony in 1892.

In one settler's memoirs, a scene is painted of a place a bit like a hamlet out of *Grimm's Fairy Tales:*

> I remember a small red hip-roofed frame structure with small windows, called the "Station". . . It had a cedar shingled roof, from which a sheet metal stove pipe protruded. The structure contained a pot-bellied heater of railway design, a coal storage compartment, a sitting bench . . . this small railway building with its heating facility and coal oil lamp was used by the colonists for many years as a meeting place and waiting room prior to train arrivals. . . . Of course, the familiar postmaster with his coal-oil lantern in one hand, and the locked heavy canvas mailbag on his shoulder was always sure to be present at train time.

My grandfather, Yehuda Joseph Eisenstein, was hired by Hirsch's forty farmers and their families in the early 1930s to be their spiritual guide, teacher and ritual slaughterer. He'd come to Canada alone, planning to bring my grandmother and their children—my mother and uncle—from Poland once he was settled. Before landing the job at Hirsch, he'd been a kind of itinerant rabbi, serving tiny Saskatchewan communities by travelling to one for a bar mitzvah, another for a wedding or to serve as a ritual slaughterer of kosher meat. Yehuda Joseph, a learned man and a natural teacher, had trained as a ritual slaughterer in Poland, with the idea that such skills were in demand in the New World. But big cities like Toronto and Montréal had more than their share of religious functionaries; it was in the small communities where he was needed, where Jewish life proved more of a struggle. Ironically, he found his first permanent post not in a typical frontier town where Jews were a tiny minority battling the pressures of assimilation, but in Hirsch, where the entire population of one hundred and fifty was Jewish—a sort of *shtetl* in the Canadian wheatland.

When my grandfather arrived at Hirsch in the early 1930s, he succeeded Marcus Berner, who proved a hard act to follow. Berner was a popular farmer-rabbi who had spent thirty-two years at Hirsch tending to his land and to the spiritual needs of his isolated community. My grandfather also arrived at a time when repeated crop failure due to drought, hail, grasshoppers, dust storms and army worms had turned a community of independent farmers into the debtors of private lenders and the wards of federal and provincial relief agencies. The colonists had become indebted as well to the JCA, and resentment between the administrators in Montréal and the farmers in Saskatchewan was a growing problem.

At Hirsch, my grandfather lived in a frame house owned by the JCA, conducted religious services and classes in a synagogue built by the organization and received his salary of fifty dollars a month from their office in Montréal. The baron's picture hung in many farmers' homes, and his birthday was celebrated with great fanfare.

The life of the Jewish settlement at Hirsch is invisible upon today's landscape, apart from the cemetery that sits by the roadside off the Trans-Canada two-lane. There, the graves have managed to stand up reasonably well against the weather; a fence rings the property, and a government plaque posted near the burial ground explains its existence, seemingly, in the middle of nowhere. Hirsch is a ghost town in the truest sense, a city of the dead, with all other signs of past habitation and community gone. Imagine, then, how difficult it is to return as a memory-tourist to such a place in an effort to discover ruins that might help us examine our own lives in light of the absence and brokenness of our ancestors' world.

The Jewish farmers' cemetery at Hirsch

My first visit to Hirsch a few years back proved fruitless. A friend and I had driven east from Calgary, turned off the Trans-Canada at Regina and dipped south toward the American border. We found the Hirsch Jewish Community Cemetery. But everything else had vanished. Houses, schools, the frame synagogue where my grandfather taught Yiddish and led the farmers in prayer. The little train platform was nowhere in sight. Even the grain elevator had been removed. I took pictures of the cemetery, but when I had them developed, they came back blank.

So a few summers later I drive again across Alberta and Saskatchewan, determined to find something more than graves beside the highway on a grassy expanse of prairie. The seed is already in and the fields are turning green with new growth, but there is still a wintry bite in the air. Torrential rains are forecast for the Hirsch area, a perfectly good excuse to forestall a second disappointment there. I decide to swing up toward Edenbridge, 150 miles north of Regina, where one of the more successful Jewish farming colonies had been. (Of the thirteen settlements scattered between Red Deer and Winnipeg, the six in Saskatchewan were the most productive.) I know that the Edenbridge synagogue is still standing, an eighty-five-year-old museum piece at the edge of a farmer's field, as well as an original homesteader's house similar to the one my grandfather lived in. I'm confident I'll find more at this destination than forgotten tombstones and the footprint of a vanished grain elevator.

When I arrive in the Edenbridge area, way up in the province's northeastern corner, the sky is promising one of the brilliant orange and violet sunsets that can only be found on the prairies, and I think there is time to look at the town site before nightfall. I have directions from a local resident as well as from an ex-colonist I'd talked to before setting out, but despite careful map work and several different approaches, the Edenbridge synagogue eludes me. I do find a tiny white clapboard church and almost convince myself it is the synagogue, refitted, the way buildings in the city are transformed from funeral homes into pubs and back again.

The car is full of road dust and lazy mosquitoes doing the backstroke along the top of the windshield. With dusk's last light turning fields of canola and flax a royal purple, I roll back to Melfort to find a motel room for the night.

On my second run down the road to Edenbridge, I have better luck finding its little synagogue in the woods. Named for a bridge the Jewish farmers helped build on the nearby Carrot River, Edenbridge was founded in 1906 by Lithuanian Jews who had lived for a time in the Transvaal. Their numbers were soon increased by the arrival of the left-leaning Gordon, Broudy and Usiskin families, whose travels had taken them from Russia to London. Mike Usiskin and his brother David had tried getting back to the land in England, but had failed at a poultry-raising scheme on London's outskirts. David came to Edenbridge first, prompted by an advertisement in a London paper touting Canada's bountiful opportunities. He lured his brother with a newspaper clipping from the Edenbridge paper picturing the cast of locals who had put on a Yiddish play.

This cultural teaser proved somewhat misleading. When Mike Usiskin joined his brother's family at Edenbridge in 1911, the challenges of homesteading—clearing land, breaking it with ox-drawn ploughs and labouring on neighbouring farms to earn a bare living—left little time for artistic pursuits. At Edenbridge, the early settlers cleared the land in teams, camping together on one family's homestead until the brush and forest had been cut down. A home would then be built from lumber purchased at nearby Star City: $23.29 for a fourteen- by eighteen-foot structure. A few more dollars bought flour to last one winter.

UNCLE MIKE, as everyone called him, was influential in local cultural life and became the community's *de facto* archivist. The memoir he wrote of his thirty-three years in the colony was published in Yiddish in 1945 by a Toronto-based firm, a publisher of leftist pamphlets enthused by the cooperative ideals of the colony. The book, an odd-looking green paperbound volume, sat on my grandparents' bookshelf in Vancouver. I remember pulling it out as a child and wondering what it could be about, with its strange cover illustration of a big-horned ox and tractor. Uncle Mike's memoir was rescued from the realm of forgotten relics when his niece, Marcia Usiskin, translated it into English. I met Marcia Usiskin in Toronto, where she told me of her years growing up on the outskirts of Winnipeg. She was six years old when her Uncle Mike, after leaving Edenbridge, came to live with her family.

"We lived rurally," Usiskin said of the family home where her uncle came to stay. "Mike had this little house on our property and I could go there every day. But he died when I was fourteen, so I've had to do a lot of work piecing things together. There was always something about the idealism of their generation—my uncle's and my father's—that I've struggled to recover."

Mike Usiskin was less interested in the hard-scrabble challenges of homesteading than in infusing his Edenbridge compatriots with his own Yiddishist and leftist ideals.

"Not that long ago I went to an Edenbridge reunion," Usiskin told me. "Everybody was given a name tag. The people I talked to told me that whenever they saw Uncle Mike coming they knew that work would have to be on hold, and they would have to just sit down and talk and listen for however long he would hang around. They always gave him the lesser jobs. But my father was wiry and much stronger. And though I think he was every bit as idealistic and every bit as committed to communal life—all this humanist stuff—he had to get on with the business of actually making a living.

"The other thing that happened to my dad was that he got married. The bachelors, when they figured they were established, by their definition—three or four of them came to Winnipeg to look for Jewish brides. But Mike remained a bachelor, and he put his energy into making Edenbridge the kind of place he thought it should be. He was always conscious that he was recording what was going on, and he kept everything he wrote. Paper was difficult to get, so he used the insides of envelopes, the backs of envelopes and paper that was waterlogged. There's a story of his buddies all sitting around one winter night, writing their poetry over a bowl of soup, when a piece of the roof fell in the soup. Even what they scribbled down that night was preserved. Mike says somewhere that he knows that the things he's writing will provide a picture of the life they were leading. I think he was one of the people who gave Edenbridge its character. The place doesn't go down in history for just being another Jewish colony like the others that became commercial. Edenbridge has its own uniqueness because of this ideal of cooperative work and the community hall. Not everything focused around the synagogue. People like my uncle and my father never imagined that they would become wealthy landowners. They were just going to lead a very rich cultural and spiritual life."

Even down at Hirsch, hundreds of miles from Edenbridge, there was word that Edenbridge's farming successes did not necessarily make for communal peace. There were the *farbrenter komunists,* my grandmother would say in Yiddish, which was more or less a euphemism for fanatical Trotskyists, and there were the more religious and conservative colonists. Like most of the world in the 1930s, politics was a subject that Edenbridge friendships lived and died by, and to Marcia Usiskin it was her ancestors' idealism that triumphed, even if Edenbridge no longer exists as a Jewish farming community.

"I think they realized after many, many years that you cannot be an island unto yourself. That they were a dot on the map, surrounded by a society whose aims and purposes were not the same as theirs. They realized they were at the mercy of taxes and mortgages and the banks who would cut off any loans. The big picture was not providing a nurturing environment for them."

But for others, the thought of Edenbridge being commemorated as a symbol of socialist idealism is galling, almost comic. I talked with Ron Rosenberg across a big table in the north Toronto ranch house that serves as the office for his development firm. Rosenberg is descended on his mother's side from the three Vickar brothers, who came by way of South Africa to become the first Jewish homesteaders at Edenbridge. His father divided his efforts between a family store and farming.

"We had the store in Brooksby, and we farmed a section in total. The store was three or four miles away from the farm, but my father was out on the farm every day. As teenagers we all went out and worked too. It was putting in the crops, taking off the crops, stooking—that's when the sheaves are put together by a binder, and you go pick them up and put them together in a little stook, as it's called. Probably the hardest work in the whole world. You're walking all the time and lifting these things, and they were heavy. Like they say, don't ask.

"In my day they already had machinery. Of course, in the early days, they didn't. How did they thrash their wheat? Well, there was always somebody had a machine in the district and went around and did this. I was just a kid when my father bought his first thrasher. And we had a tractor. I ploughed and did all the things you do on a tractor. I guess we started kind of early because at fourteen or fifteen I was already driving the tractors and ploughing."

When I asked Rosenberg about divisions in the community, his curiosity was piqued.

"Now, who told you that? Because this is something that very few people talk about in these so-called books, and I had it in mind to talk about this to you. My reminiscences can only start in the late twenties, but even as a child you knew, you heard what was going on. And, yes, the Jewish community at Edenbridge was a typical microcosm of the world. You had all degrees of political thinking."

Rosenberg drew a map on a sheet of paper, dividing the colony's land along a township survey line. He pointed out the pocket north of this line, where you had what Rosenberg called "left wingers, communists, plain and simple. They were a minority, but like all minorities who are self-righteous, they were extremely vocal." Next Rosenberg sketched in the southerly tracts, where his family farmed.

"The Vickars," he said of his mother's family, "they sort of ran the show. They were active in the synagogue and in politics. My Uncle Dave was the reeve for twenty-one years. They were orthodox—not ultra-super-duper orthodox, but they went to *shul* on Saturdays, and they didn't drive on the Sabbath. Now, I never saw it, but I know there were animosities between my family and the communist families. It really was a divided community. Don't forget, in the 1930s, when Stalin came to power, there were an awful lot of Jews who thought he was the salvation. That there'd be one great big wonderful world. And these people were very pro-Russia. There was a song they used to sing called 'Bim Bom Bom.' It began, 'Lenin, Trotsky, *di gabonim,*' which meant 'the great men.'

"Now we've got this cottage industry, people writing books about the Edenbridge community and the other colonies. And, oh boy, sometimes they make it sound so glamorous and so wonderful—all these Jews farming and it couldn't be better. I would go to the meetings when these writers talked and introduce myself as one of the last living relics. I explained that I didn't want to abuse anybody's great stories, but they're all romanticized and idealized. Your grandmother will tell you the romantic idealism that's portrayed by the historical societies and in all these books is a lot of bull, really."

This interplay of the ideal and the real, of a sense of triumph and complete defeat lurks behind every account of life in the Jewish prairie farming colonies. In 1942, Gabrielle Roy, then a young journalist and not yet a writer of fiction about francophone Canada, called on Mike Usiskin. She was travelling across the country by train, visiting Mennonite, Hutterite and Jewish colonists along the way. When Roy saw Edenbridge, it was a bustling community of family farms with its own school, which served the entire district.

Roy saw the Eden in Edenbridge, a place where women drew water at the well and men hitched their horses for the day's work. Over this idyllic scene, the sun cast "its golden rays on the proud, thick-standing heads of grain."

But as the children of farmers went off to university and city jobs, the old-timers found it harder and harder to keep up. Nor could they effectively compete with larger farming operations that used expensive modern technology to harvest huge areas. Still, Marcia Usiskin insisted that the gradual abandonment of Edenbridge by its inhabitants in the years following the Second World War did not represent a defeat for men like her father and Uncle Mike. "They realized after many years," she said, "that you cannot be an island unto yourself. They did, after all, succeed in their original goal of leaving Russia and coming to Canada, where they had an opportunity to work the land."

IT MAY HAVE BEEN the secularist ideology of many of the settlers and their children that sealed the communities' fate. Unlike Mennonite and Hutterite farmers who passed on an insular world-view to their children, the Jewish settlers encouraged their children to look outward and explore the world, which is exactly what they did.

Though I have been told that an original homesteader's house remains not far from the synagogue site at Edenbridge, I am still flabbergasted to find the two-storey frame building that stands on what was Israel Broudy's farm. Its floor has settled so it rides the slope of the land like a saddle on a horse. Descendants of the original settlers have gone to great lengths to preserve the synagogue, which stands quite square and sports a new coat of white paint. By contrast, the house slouches beside a raised gravel road

The shell of a settler's home at Edenbridge, at the edge of a farmer's field

and a broad expanse of ploughed field. Inside it, against one wall, a steep and decrepit set of stairs leads to the second floor. A hole in the floorboards marks where the stovepipe was once fixed.

Across the road the old wooden synagogue could be a mirage made of heat and sun, a vision out of Chagall's Russian villagescapes plunked down in the Canadian wheatland. Its modest sanctuary is built tight, like a ship, out of buttery-coloured planks. The wood is so dry when I visit that prairie gusts play the structure as if it were some marvelous woodwind instrument. From the raised platform where the rabbi stood in the old days (the building remained in use into the 1960s), there is a view over miles and miles of north Saskatchewan farm land. One can easily imagine how belief—fired by the fear of disaster and thankfulness for plenty—would have thrived in the hearts of worshippers as they gazed out at their fields.

The trials of settling the prairie, coupled with the demands of religious customs suited to life in European towns and cities, has inspired numerous Hollywood farces. In *The Frisco Kid,* Gene Wilder plays a European newcomer to the American West who is seen tracking a prairie

The beautifully preserved wooden synagogue at Edenbridge

chicken while decked out in his *shtetl* gabardines. As the bird eludes him he chants, "I'm not going to kill you. I'm just going to eat you." (Jewish ritual law requires animals to be caught, not shot, before being slaughtered.) In *Blazing Saddles*, Mel Brooks sends up the idea of Jewish frontiersmen by having his Indian characters speak Yiddish. Though Hollywood stretched the truth, it did reflect the dramatic gap between Old and New World customs and between expectation and reality.

Though the Canadian government was happy to send these Europeans out west, they showed mixed faith in the homesteaders' long-term success. Indeed, it was Sir John A. Macdonald's belief that the Jews would "all at once go in for peddling and politics." He was proved wrong. Through the hard years of crop failure, which began in the Hirsch and Hoffer area even before the onset of the Dirty Thirties, Jewish farmers stayed on the land in average or slightly better numbers than the general population. A 1938 article in the *Montréal Standard* noted that 40 per cent of the Jewish farmers' sons had left the land, while the figure for the total population was slightly higher.

But still, many were unwilling to endure the hardship. At Wapella the patriarch of the Bronfman dynasty farmed for a time, but in a photograph taken in 1899, Ekiel Bronfman has the detached appearance and set jaw of a man who knows he is on his way somewhere else.

FROM EDENBRIDGE I travel south through the rolling Qu'Apelle Valley, past Regina, Weyburn and the coal mining town of Estevan, to meet Usher Berger, one of the last Jewish farmers. Berger's farm is just north of the American border, west of Hirsch, on the site where the Jewish farm colony of Hoffer once thrived. Named for the family that ran the most successful farm in the area, Hoffer boasted forty-five farms at its peak in 1916, with a population of 147 and more than 10,800 acres under cultivation. In 1917, Hoffer's inhabitants organized the Jewish Farmer's Cooperative Union, a precursor of the wheat pools that thrived during the 1920s.

Berger is not only the last Jew farming at Hoffer, and so the keeper of the community's stories, he pretty much owns the history of the place by virtue of holding title to a good deal of the historic land. His house sits on Israel Hoffer's original homestead, and his farm includes the homestead his father registered in 1909, as well as the old Hoffer cemetery, where nine of the community's elders are buried.

My first communication from Berger had come in the form of a neatly typed letter, which he sent in response to my phone messages asking if we could meet. Bearing a return address from Berger's winter home in Regina, the letter read

Dear Mr. Ravvin:

I have received both your May 1st. letter addressed to Oungre and the one dated May 5th. which you sent to Regina.

I have been very busy with seeding, but this is almost completed now.

I look forward to your visit in June. Unless it is very wet I should be on the farm on the 6th. and 9th. and if you contact me a day or two ahead of time, we should be able to arrange to meet. I am alone on the farm, and outdoors most of the time, so the best time to telephone would be between 12 and 1pm or after 10pm. I wish you every success with your articles on Jewish pioneer history, and hope that any information I may have will prove useful to you.

Yours truly,
Usher Berger

Calling from a motel pay phone as I make my way south from Edenbridge, I reach Berger to let him know I'll be in his area the following day. Scribbled on the bottom of his letter is my seemingly worthless transcription of his directions on how to find him once I've hit the province's southerly tip.

The following morning is grey and muddy, and I find myself bumping around Berger's farm in his pick-up. That there has been a cottage industry in recording local prairie history is made obvious by the well-planned tour Berger gives me of what had been the Hoffer farm. I am by no means the first to come chasing ghosts. As he noses his truck over the soft rise and fall of the land, Berger gives me an idea of what life was like for the early homesteaders.

In order to retain title to their land, new farmers were obliged to live on it for six months of each year and farm a certain amount of it. At first, in 1905 or 1906, when they were choosing and breaking in their farms, Berger's father and his compatriots were totally isolated. They lived in shacks they built themselves, owned no machinery or livestock and received no support from any agency, governmental or philanthropic. It was a fifty-mile walk to Estevan for supplies.

"Once, in the winter," Berger says, "my father and his friends went off, and when they got back the snow had completely covered their shacks. They couldn't find them." Berger has stayed close to the surrounding sections since his father died young in 1933. His mother managed the land with the help of a hard-working hired man until Berger began upgrading and expanding, building on the resources his father had left.

"We had a little bit of money," he tells me, "and I would go to auctions where farmers who'd bought new machinery were selling off this old junk, so I bought horses and obsolete machinery. I can remember ploughing 120 acres. It took a whole month to do it, and I can go out in my four-wheel-drive tractor today and be done in no time. Almost every time I'm out on the land I remember that. But the pace of the country is altogether different now. In the old days you were satisfied with smaller acreage. But there was always a push. I don't know if it's me or what, but I get bigger machines, I get out of cattle, and I think I'm gonna be on easy street, and I come out here and still work my bloody head off. I used to work all this land myself. Now I've rented out six quarters, so I'm only working two sections of land, and I'm still working my head off. When it rains I should be taking it easy, but this has to be fixed and that has to be repaired. There's always something. I'm sixty-seven years old. I've got to start looking at the day when I'll have to let it go."

When Berger married in 1961, there were only two or three Jewish farmers left on the land, but the depopulation of the Hoffer area was not merely a question of the children of original farmers fleeing to the cities to get an education or seek a Jewish partner. He sees the collapse of the area as part of a larger phenomenon that has transformed rural Canada.

"Well, first of all, good roads and good automobiles were the start. When your method of transport was horses, you had a town every five or six miles apart. But the most distance you wanted between two towns was ten miles because a storekeeper could expect the trade within that area. Once the roads improved and people started to get cars, they'd go around and shop where they could get the cheapest price. The storekeepers were facing quite a bit more competition as people would get their groceries at stores which, because of volume, could sell them cheaper. And then, I don't know what was the thinking of the government or of the JCA or of anybody else, that on half a section of land you could make a living. You could make a starving, but you couldn't make a living. So they started moving out. The neighbour would pick up the land when it became available. As the farms got bigger, the population got scarce. So whereas a storekeeper could make a living when he had the trade from everyone living on every half-section or three-quarters of land, when people started farming a section and a half or two sections, where was he going to get his trade from? Now it's just getting worse. With this austerity and the deficit, these little towns that had a nursing home and a hospital where people could retire to, the hospitals are being closed down and they're going to have to retire where there's a bigger centre. So the rural population is going down, down, down."

This is a sad end to the heroic efforts of Hoffer's early farmers. But Berger suggests that without the funds contributed by the Baron de Hirsch's Jewish Colonization Association, the settlement would have floundered almost as soon as its founders began ploughing.

"The JCA built them a house, a barn and a chicken coop," Berger says. "They bought them machines, horses, chickens, and probably some cows." In addition to providing an influx of capital into the local communities, the JCA paid its municipal taxes at a time when few could, helping to maintain such local services as the much-needed country doctor.

"I can remember going to school in dust storms that were just like in the Sahara Desert," Berger tells me. "In the thirties, there wasn't one person in the municipality whose sole income was agriculture and who wasn't on relief, which today is called welfare. Big. Small. Everybody."

I HAD DONE WELL to go first to Edenbridge, with its museum piece of a synagogue, and then to Hoffer, where the memories preserved by Usher Berger gave the landscape back its voice. When I arrive at Hirsch, the big sky is heavy, the colour of slate, and the town site is just as I had seen it on my first visit a few years before: a desolate, windswept stretch of wild grass.

Before he managed to bring his wife and children to Hirsch from

Poland, my grandfather lived alone for three years amidst a sea of sardine tins and Yiddish newspapers. He wasn't unhappy there, visiting with farmers who brought chickens to him to be killed, making calls to nearby towns like Estevan that had too few Jews to support their own rabbi. In the little school at Hirsch, he taught the farmer's children about Jewish culture, trying to interest them in customs that must have seemed as foreign to them as a heat wave in January. He liked the Jewish farmers and admired the way they faced the unpredictability of their lives while striving to preserve generations-old customs from Europe. Yet it took my grandmother less than a year from the time of her arrival to convince her husband that Hirsch was no place for a young family. He began looking for work in a bigger Jewish centre, moving his family first to Yorkton and then to Vancouver.

"It was one street, no sidewalks," my grandmother recalled of Hirsch, circa 1935. "With three stores. Everyone was jealous, saying, 'Why did you go to him to buy?'" The children came in from the farms to go to school, and the farmers rode oxcarts or horse-pulled wagons to attend synagogue on Saturday morning. It was one of these horse-borne Sabbath-goers who told my grandmother, "Whatever we are, we're still Jews," a line she would repeat to me fifty years later with a touch of pride as well as wonder in her voice. She'd only been at Hirsch nine months in total, and seemed, in recollection, to barely believe it had all happened. In my grandmother's memories of Hirsch there was little sentiment and no idealized reminiscence of a great adventure in the New World. As an introduction to the place, she recalled one farmer among the contingent who greeted her at the train station, asking, "Why did your husband bring you over here?" She remembered such wicked cold in the winter that after the stove had been lit the frozen walls of their house began to thaw and water ran onto the floor. There was much to complain about, but there was also balm for the soul. It was at Hirsch that my grandmother learned to bake bread and cakes, to pluck and cook a chicken. Amid the hardship and isolation, work was not only a necessity but a distraction from the memories of family left behind in Europe.

Big sky and flatland on the southern prairie near Hirsch

Today, the Hirsch town site, a few miles north of the Souris River Valley, might be thought of as part of a wild, outdoor museum to the past. Old maps will tell you where the Roche Percee band left their pictographs on sandstone hoodoos and where the Romanian and Russian Jews buried their dead. The clearest marks on the land today, beside the roads crisscrossing the prairie, are old mining pits. Not far from Hirsch, at Bienfait, elevator shafts remain, which were dug deep into the land's rich coal seams, with horizontal shafts running out from them. Underground, horses hauled heavy loads in the near dark.

Beyond these markings, the relics of the past are sparse. Standing on the roadside near the place called Hirsch, I am overwhelmed by a sense of all that's vanished. As I stand by the Hirsch cemetery in late afternoon, a yellow line of light appears on the horizon. Beneath the light is the dark line of the land, marked only by the fast-departing silver and redlit back end of an eighteen-wheeler pulling a load of oil. Anything else man-made is overwhelmed by a big, dark, late-afternoon sky—miles high and wide, heavy with a rain that refuses to fall.

Buying Leo Dinner

ASTINGS STREET used to be the main stem of downtown Vancouver. Housewives shopped there for fish, and professional men walked along it to work, serious hats on their heads. Today, newspaper reports tell us that the postal code that includes Hastings Street is the poorest in Canada. Journalists go in search of the famous "shooting galleries" that give them the right to dub the area around Hastings the "inner city," a term only recently heard in Canada. In their reports, the old downtown of Vancouver takes on the character of a kind of black hole, mocking the beauty of the rest of the city.

To judge for yourself, take a stroll down West Hastings, past haggard street walkers who will pay passersby a low-key but steady attention. Sometimes a prolonged stare precedes a request for a handout. The surrounding façades of once-proud office blocks have slid into dereliction, and the new development along the eastern edge of False Creek is built like a fortress, turning its massive brick face against what's known as Vancouver's downtown east side. To a large extent, the divide between down-and-out Vancouver and the rest of the city is never crossed.

There is, however, one surprising side effect to the disinterest of the rest of the city in what it has come to view as its own "inner city." Leftovers of an almost extinct Vancouver bohemia can be found among the boarded up banks, the pigeon-spattered war monuments, the great old warehouse blocks that flank the rail line tying the city to its port. On these streets one can find the makings of artists, writers and counterculture characters who have viewed the old downtown as a kind of alternative zone, a part of the city that hasn't yet been given over to international tourism and bears no resemblance whatsoever to an urban park.

This is the vantage that author Norman Levine chose in the late 1950s, when he described Vancouver in his memoir *Canada Made Me.* Already the area around Hastings Street had slid into skid-row scruffiness. Yet Levine found a certain peace and pleasure in the street's special burnt-out quality:

> I liked it from the beginning. . . . I asked a taxi driver to take me to a small hotel. He brought me to one in Hastings near Main. An old man in a shabby brown suit was behind the desk. . . . He said I could have a room at $2.50 a night . . . most of the rooms on the floor were occupied by women. They were not attractive, nor young. When I saw them in the daytime downstairs, waiting for the elevator or shopping in the Chinese store, they appeared in a state of stupor, as if they were perpetually drunk.

One of the last outposts of this alternative city was the Or Gallery at 112 West Hastings, an address that once housed Perel Brothers Tailors, the clothing business of two Polish Holocaust survivors. The Perels made a living selling cloth coats and leather handbags, some of which they manufactured themselves. Their shop was the kind of business that served the downtown when the nearby streets were Vancouver's central shopping and business district. What remained of the tailor shop is the *-or* in tailors, which supplied the gallery with its sign, along with a few abandoned industrial sewing machines on the building's upper floor.

The building's owner, Moshe Perel, liked the idea that his real estate, stuck in a dead neighbourhood, might serve the needs of artists. The Or Gallery is one of the many enterprises, including artists' live-in studios, that appeared on the streets around West Hastings to take advantage of cheap rents and the bohemian atmosphere of an old and failed city centre. The Or's curator, Reid Shier, told me that for a short time, in the late 1980s and early '90s, the area was "infested with studios and galleries, most of which have moved out by now."

"It's an example of reverse gentrification," Shier says. "The area was shit but livable, so artists moved in. The area became worse, and artists moved out. Not the normal equation, but I think it can be pretty much attributed to the drug trade being pushed onto Hastings and away from Gastown, downtown and Strathcona, which border the area on three sides. Because there's no occupancy, there's no complaints, and not heard, not seen, it would seem."

Not many blocks from the notorious postal code is some of Canada's most startling and valuable real estate. If you look at a map of downtown Vancouver, you can see that it is a kind of island. Like many port cities, the surrounding bays and harbours leave a few valuable outcroppings and peninsulas for people to live on. It's the east side of the downtown that failed—the oldest part of the settlement along the Burrard Inlet, which was originally called Granville. As early as the late fifties, everyone who could was moving their businesses and offices west, toward what we now call the West End.

This precinct of the downtown is only about ten blocks from the old centre of town at Main and Hastings, but the two parts of the city could not be more different. The West End, bordered by English Bay and Stanley Park, has become one of the most inviting, though high-priced neighbourhoods in the country. A fifteen minute walk away, the area surrounding the Or Gallery is a disaster. Shier tells dreary stories of the area's complete eclipse; with the disappearance of almost every traditional business, the streets take on a ghostly frontier craziness at night.

When the Or mounted a retrospective of Cuban Art, one of the contingencies among the visitors was made up of Mexican and Salvadorean drug dealers, who were excited to find an outpost of Latino culture on their beat. For weeks after the show had been replaced by something conceptual in which an artist created an installation using his hair, the

Mexicans and Salvadoreans would come in and ask, "What's with this hair? Where are the Cubans? Are they coming back?"

"They went home," Shier told them. "Show's over."

Not long afterward, the show was truly over for a young woman who was working the night shift in a cheque cashing outlet down the street from the Or. A man convinced her to let him into her booth and killed her for the cash on hand. Investigators guessed that the only reason she put herself in such danger was that she knew her killer.

The first thing I knew about downtown Vancouver was that a great-uncle of mine was murdered there in his second-hand store on West Cordova Street, about a block from the eventual location of the Or Gallery. This happened in the early 1960s, when a murder in Vancouver was big news. My mother, having moved to Calgary, remembers hearing over the radio that a pawnshop owner had been killed on West Cordova, but she didn't catch the name of the victim, and it didn't occur to her that it might be her Uncle Izzy who'd made the CBC's hourly news report.

Izzy called his store Reliable Loan Pawnbrokers, and it was one of a number of businesses that took advantage of the low rent and walk-by from The Army and Navy and Woodwards stores up the block. Izzy worked long hours—sometimes being spelled by his wife or his young sons—and he made a reasonable, though not spectacular living selling used men's suits, luggage, jewelry and sporting goods to Vancouver's working poor.

In a way, he was carrying on a second-hand tradition in Vancouver's downtown that went back to the city's earliest days, when miners came to the Gastown area off Cordova to get outfitted for their next stint up in the Klondike. With his earnings from the store, Izzy managed to buy a few modest properties on Vancouver's west side, the crowning achievement of a family man, relatively new to the city, who was trying to abandon his Europeanness in favour of whatever a post-war Vancouver style might be. In the small-town Polish life he'd left behind, among other trades, Izzy had made a living going from village to village with a wooden box full of glass on his back and a sharpened blade he used to cut farm women a window.

My great-uncle was one of the liberating influences in my mother's Vancouver childhood. He'd come to Canada before his brother's family, and he knew better than my mom's own parents what would make a Canadian kid happy. He bought her and her brothers ice skates, and he would come by in his Austin Minor to take them for a summer swim at the University's Olympic-size pool. Izzy, family legend has it, was a smiler, a life-enjoyer; he even had a reputation among the rummies who congregated near his store as a good-hearted Jew. You could get a quarter out of him most times you asked.

But his popularity didn't stop his luck from running out one Saturday afternoon. He was in his store alone, something he'd become leery of even in those relatively innocent days before Vancouver became a big city. Two men came into the store and demanded the day's receipts. No one saw what happened next, but from the mess in the store, it appeared that my great-uncle put up a good fight. Though we bemoan the increase of the number of handguns in our cities, what was done to Izzy with a blunt object was not for the faint-hearted. He was alive when he was found, but barely, and I have a vividly imagined picture of his round face, spectacles knocked off, his blond hair sticky with his own blood, his suit vest buttoned up over his battered body.

Because the pawnshop had been in space owned by the man who ran the Army and Navy stores, a reward was offered by my great-uncle's prominent landlord. And the reward turned the trick. Within a week a woman came forward to tell the police that one of the murderers had boasted to her about doing the job. He had even shown her a wristwatch he'd nabbed in his hasty exit from the place, which happened to belong to Izzy's wife. This tip quickly led the police to the second man as well. It turned out that my great-uncle's killers were young native men recently released from prison. They went directly back there, for twenty-five years without a chance of parole. I heard, not long after I moved to Vancouver, that they'd been released, and I wondered if they ever made their way past the building that had housed my uncle's store.

It's strange then that when I moved to downtown Vancouver I rarely thought of this grisly family story out of the city's annals of urban crime. True, I lived in a different part of the downtown. West Cordova by then was part of the old, troubled centre of the city that had settled into skid-row failure. The Army and Navy and Woodwards were the last of the important economic anchors, and Woodwards itself would soon bite the dust, leaving little beyond the blocks of flophouses, well-greased cafés, cheque cashing agencies and derelict warehouses. In the early 1980s, Gastown was still a rather conspicuous failure. Tourists couldn't really be convinced to come down to the corner of Cordova and Carrall to buy a Cowichan sweater in full view of a troupe of sad rummies urinating against a brick wall. But touristy shops—offering knick-knacks like the Vancouver bear, so famous now as the gift President Clinton gave Monica Lewinsky, were getting by as best they could.

When I moved to Vancouver to attend university in 1981, I found myself drawn to the remnants of the vaunted counterculture that lurked behind boarded storefronts on Carrall Street, behind the quizzical, joking expressions of unusual professors I met at U.B.C. who still did bohemi-an things like hang out with students, run offset presses out of their east-side basements, bring strangers into their backyard for a fragrant joint under the pear tree or take a stray home for Passover Seder only to dis-cover that the pretty young lady was really a ravenous, tubercular man in drag. These were the days when the part of downtown Vancouver called the West End was an affordable renters' neighbourhood. This was before Expo '86, and the West End had not been affected by any substantial redevelopment since the early 1970s, when the most recent zoning free-for-all had seen a number of high-rises replace the old houses and three-storey walk-up apartment blocks. I had the good fortune to live near Stanley Park, Lost Lagoon, a quick walk from Robson Street, the Public Library and movie theatres, when the area had a modicum of calm and stability. You didn't wonder each time you walked out in the morning what building had been slated to be knocked down.

When change is a constant in a neighbourhood, there are no regulars, no local rhythms, no steady pleasures. In the early and mideighties, the West End had all of these. My block of Broughton Street was bisected by Comox and Pendrell, which run down toward English Bay. The alleyway beside our building was quiet, though you often saw down-and-outers diving into dumpsters in the hope of discovering a half-eaten sandwich, discarded clothes they might be able to use or junked appliances.

Up on Davie Street the city had not yet decided how to deal with a local attraction: large numbers of hookers who roamed the back streets and alleys, leading thousands of drivers downtown to simply cruise and gawk. Men, alone and in pairs, hung out the windows of Camaros and pick-ups, shouting inanities. A movie called *Hookers on Davie,* about one of the more flamboyant transvestite hookers, got a good deal of press. The film's most compelling character was immediately familiar as the long-legged, dark-haired figure I often saw crossing from one all-night restaurant to another, tripping on high heels across the rain-slick pavement. When the movie was old news I heard that he'd been murdered by a john wielding a claw hammer in the midst of an aborted trick.

This leggy fixture of Davie Street was, of course, a bohemian fringe dweller. A flaunter of rules. An artist working out his own system of desire while the city's influential and invisible powers were busy imagining a way to transform the downtown into something new, which would attract more tourists and please the eye, not of its inhabitants, but of the rest of the world. In time, the hookers were evicted from West End streets, while the entire neighbourhood was turned into another kind of whore, a beautiful precinct devoted to luxuries you can't get at home.

I've not lived in Vancouver for more than a decade, though it's hard to believe. The place has remained so resonant and important to me. During the years I lived in Toronto, I tried to spend a month of each year visiting Vancouver. Made up of a combination of two or three trips in the winter and summer, this month of walking, visiting friends and maintaining old family patterns made the city and its neighbourhoods seem close at hand, if not completely recoverable. On nearly every visit, I drove or walked to the West End apartment buildings I'd lived in on Broughton and Haro streets, sometimes taking a friend along to peek in the window to see whose stuff was in place where mine had been.

These were nostalgic visits, failed efforts to recapture my sense of place, my confidence that the city was mine. While I was back, I would weed my grandmother's garden—first in the yard of the house she'd lived in since wartime and then around the patio of the condominium she moved to in her middle eighties, when the house became more work than the freedom it gave her was worth. One summer visit, in part to help her move out of the house, I did quick work removing two old rose bushes she was attached to, bagging the roots and driving the plants up the street to her new place, where I dropped them into sandy holes before the representative of the Thai conglomerate that had bought her house called me what I was: a thief, but a thief of memories.

Depending on the season of my visit, I undertook a different reconnaissance mission to find out how the downtown was faring. With one friend I took long walks to the eastern port side of town, which has been transformed by the Plaza of Nations and the Pan Pacific Hotel made famous by Boris Yeltsin's summit visit to the city. With another friend I'd walk the Stanley Park seawall and take in the Park's green beauty as we ruminated about our work and the city's ups and downs.

It became clear to me that it was impossible to maintain any real connection with Vancouver from a distance. The city was changing too quickly. In a decade it had taken on a kind of cosmopolitan glitter, a broad-shouldered American confidence; and though there is no development so outlandish that can completely obliterate the wonder of living on a mellow coastal outpost surrounded by ocean and mountains, every neighbourhood—not just the downtown—has shed an older skin in favour of something new. On summer visits throughout the nineties, I often sat in the window of a Starbucks on Robson Street at Bute—the store looking south that catches the sun, not the one kitty-corner in the old Manhattan Apartments that is darker, though equally busy.

ONE MORNING, with a newspaper folded beside a coffee, I look up at the crowd gathered like patients in an overbooked doctor's office and catch sight of Leo, an acquaintance I connect with my old West End. He doesn't seem to notice me, so I sit and watch him stare out at the street with his full mug of coffee steaming in the sunlight. He sits so still, he might be meditating.

WHEN LEO AND I were neighbours on Broughton Street in the West End, pockets of what Vancouver had been like in the sixties and seventies could be found everywhere. On West Fourth by Burrard, downtown on the fringes of Gastown, and on the east side, of course, people exhibited ways of living and being unkonwn to a middle-class kid from Calgary, where a curious homogeneity reigns eternal. Communities of artists, down-and-outers, and political and sexual revolutionaries of all stripes hung their flags out proudly. Their dress included equal parts of carnival impresario and grave digger—no Gore-tex for them. They chose restaurants without a liquor licence so they could bring their own in a paper bag, and they patronized carefully chosen bars that were the guild clubs of cab drivers or mariners who accepted nonmembers with a wary, disinterested silence.

I was fascinated by this variety, this casual flaunting of everyday rituals. But I realize I was watching a kind of ending. I moved to the West End at a time when the great days of Vancouver bohemia were, if not dead, quickly passing. The Gabriola—the mansion the Rogers sugar fortune built, which had been a rooming house in the 1970s and had harboured all sorts of spice-growing, incense-burning drop-outs—was a Hy's Steakhouse. (Could anything be less bohemian than a Hy's Steakhouse, that Calgary-founded sirloin-sizzling counterpart to Trader Vic's?) The old deco apartment blocks, beloved of tenants with an eye for elaborate interiors, were giving way to massive grey high-rises, the kind developers advertise in the newspaper as "Concrete Building." Obviously, there are people out there who find this feature a drawing point.

I lived with my brother on Broughton Street, not far from Stanley

*Michael Kluckner's 1989 watercolour of the Gainsborough's west-facing façade;
the dark frame house in the foreground—which obscures the view of Leo's
house—has been transformed into a condominium with all the fixings*

Park, in a six-storey brick apartment block called the Gainsborough,
which at the time still harboured a number of Vancouver's crazy, magic
people. At night, giants could be seen ascending the front steps trailing
boas. The rental manager's son, Thor, practiced his saxophone on the
stoop. My brother and I befriended the couple next door, who had obviously chosen their apartment for its old-fashioned elegance, the high ceil-
ings and foot-deep window sills you could actually sit on to watch the
street. Ray, the artist of the pair, had painted a Rousseau-ish mural on his
dining room wall. The big kitchen offered plenty of room for a hutch,
where Rick—a frustrated Jewish mama's boy from Toronto (the first such
specimen I'd ever met)—raised rabbits. Parties were habitual among the
tenants, and my brother and I, none too skilled at hospitality, even threw
a few memorable ones ourselves.

Leo, my fixture of old Vancouver, did not live in the Gainsborough.
His room, which I never actually stepped into, was rented in a tumble-

Rooming house on
Broughton Street
behind its holly
bushes

down, stucco-sprayed boarding house that sat across the alley in full view
of my big living room window. Leo's house mates were a fascinating collection of what you might call lumpenbohemia. These were men—and
yes, they were all men—who did no apparent thing all day, day after day.
One played a penny whistle of some kind so tunelessly that my brother
and I found it nearly impossible to concentrate on anything when he was
at it, beside complaining to each other about his tunelessness.

But it was because of this mysterious whistler that I met Leo. He was
the most alert-looking by far of the rooming house's tenants. He kept
himself busy in a garage studio, where he worked under a single bare bulb.
It was also within view of my apartment window. Driftwood disappeared
into the garage and reappeared on the porch, on the roof of the house,
sometimes in the trash, as comic, almost surreal carved figures.

I introduced myself to Leo one summer morning, with the wind in the elms and the shadows long and creamy crawling down the alleyway, as he rested on the porch with a paperback. I asked if he knew who the guy was who blew his whistle so annoyingly.

"I do," he answered in careful, accented English. "He is practicing to be in the symphony."

Leo said this in such a perfectly deadpan way that he defused all my interest in solving the whistler problem. Instead, I wanted to get to know this man who could turn an uptight neighbour's complaint into a joke by way of straight-faced irony.

Leo the Sculptor turned out to be the most manifestly bohemian soul I would meet during the years I lived in Vancouver's West End. He was, in fact, born not far from the true geographical source of bohemianism, in Prague. He told me the kind of life story that was so fantastic it had to be true. As a youth he'd apprenticed to a master sculptor and trained to carve altar pieces, but as his mentor sunk into drink and debilitation, Leo gave up on the Old World and set out on one of those mythical walks across Europe—modelled, I imagine, on Chagall's abandonment of Vitebsk, or Brancusi's departure from the backwoods of Romania for Paris. My sculptor friend managed not only to walk out of communist Europe but also to cross the Atlantic and then North America, landing in the beaten-up rooming house that stood on Broughton between Comox and Pendrell.

When he wasn't lounging with a paperback or strolling or just minding his own business, he worked feverishly at his art in the long dark garage beneath the rooming house porch. Most often he worked on the smaller pieces that were scattered around the yard, and more rarely, he made progress on a giant crucified Jesus he was carving. The figure was so large that its parts had never been put together. Now and then I saw Leo drag an upper arm or a thigh into the sun to check its proportions, but I don't think he ever assembled and viewed the entire figure.

As we got to know each other better, I found that Leo had a wonderful lackadaisical attitude about life. He entered sculpting competitions at the last minute with wild proposals, and he had made an agreement with a downtown school to carve a surreal jungle gym for the kids. He found me as entertaining as I did him (he couldn't understand how anyone could sit for so long at a kitchen table, pouring over lecture notes and readings for class), and we developed a predictable routine in which I listened to stories of his wanderings, playing the patient Canadian stump to his Boho magician's worldliness.

I studied Leo's example because secretly, alongside my disciplined student's schedule, supposedly a prelude to safe professional life, I was hoping to create a counter-life, a subterranean existence that might offer release from responsibilities I had no interest in, from the middle-class care and seriousness I applied to my studies and relationships. I wanted to become a writer of some kind, a chronicler of lives like Leo's. And to do so, it seemed to me, a certain amount of bohemian coffee-swilling and nose-thumbing at the nine-to-five world was required.

As part of my initiation into this counter-life, I went often to the Classical Joint, a now-defunct jazz emporium on Carrall Street in Gastown, a block from the Or Gallery and not far from West Cordova, where my great-uncle was killed. There I scribbled in little notebooks and watched, waiting for service, while more people emerged from the back room than entered the front door. The Classical Joint was the closest you could get in Vancouver to a Greenwich Village coffee house. I think if you gave the right sort of wink you got a shot of whiskey in your tea, but otherwise hot chocolate and chicory flavoured coffee were the drinks of choice. The decor resembled a furnished garage. The tables by the windows were on raised platforms, where people huddled in their coats over a game of chess, and the place was small enough that the tables up front by the band had about six inches clearance if one of the musicians decided to pull out a trombone.

Once, I saw Joe Rosenblatt read long stuttering poems about bumblebees. Sometimes, I brought along picture books to flip through that portrayed Vancouver's quieter years, the 1950s and early '60s, when the surrounding area still comprised a neighbourhood, albeit one populated largely by middle-aged men in fedoras with sweater vests under their sport coats. I wrote a lot of crap. But somewhere along the way I wrote a story in which Leo's life appeared, slightly distorted for purposes I cannot explain and set against the backdrop of a Prague drawn from the newspapers, for I had not been to Europe. I sold the story for a remarkable sum—one thousand dollars—and a friend with a sharp sense of humour asked me if I was going to take Leo to dinner on the money I'd earned off his life.

WHEN LEO LOOKS ACROSS the coffee bar and catches me watching him, his expression changes as he realizes that my face is familiar. He recognizes me as his old neighbour and I go over to reacquaint. Leo tells me I've gained weight, which I immediately take as a slight. I'd abandoned Bohemia— what little of it I'd partaken of—and was eating well. But nothing has changed for Leo as far as I can tell. He'd been up all night preparing a proposal for a public sculpture that is planned for the new downtown Public Library. He looks like he's been up all night. I probably look like I've been asleep for days. He is hyping himself up on coffee so he can work through another long December afternoon. He is pleased to hear I've published a novel since we'd last seen each other, and I promise I'll send him a copy (in lieu of the dinner I never treated him to). Then I leave him alone with his resolute, haggard, coffee-fueled inner world and return to my straight, riskless, slightly anxious business. I don't ask what Leo has to say about the transformations of his downtown, where the old Public Library turned into a combination Virgin Records store and Planet Hollywood, and the tourists stand politely behind a velvet rope at two in the afternoon.

Most of the old Britishy fish-and-chips joints, flower shops, corner groceries, bookshops, shoe stores and dry cleaners are gone. These weren't necessarily things you loved or even liked when they were there, but they presented neighbourly possibilities. Also gone: modest Sezchuan restaurants and little Chinese groceries where you could buy a bag of sunflower seeds, the old Café Zen on Howe, a weird den of mixed clientele made up of bohemian do-nothings, dog-pound staff cutting work and lawyers over from the courthouse for lunch to check out the action.

Robson Street, where Leo and I had prowled after a muffin and newspaper, has become an approximation of Rodeo Drive or any of the other internationalized strips given over to the irresistible draw of foreign exchange, suburban expense accounts, teens with new cars they want to show off at magic hour when the light hits the paint job just so.

Did Leo resent the memory of Expo '86 as I did? And did he remember the summer before it as a kind of twilight hour, when the city was more or less hypeless, unfazed by the need to attain world class status, when people like Leo and me simply viewed the West End as our neighbourhood? As a place to live and work, where the rest of the city's citizens visited once in a while to see a movie or park on the way to English Bay. In the old days, there were plenty of Vancouverites who didn't even bother with that. But somehow the suburban ethic has tarnished. People want to come back to the centre. And those who don't want to live downtown at least want to shop there. Some are even willing to stand in line at Planet Hollywood and daydream about Demi Moore's pectoral development. But what's that got to do with living on Bute or Broughton?

THE OR GALLERY, like Leo's rooming house, is a shadow thrown by a city that no longer stands. The gallery has produced some of Vancouver's best known art. Reid Shier tells me that Jeff Wall, whose gigantic backlit photo tableaux of Vancouver scenes are among Canada's best-known contemporary artworks, did most of his early work at the Or (one of his earliest pieces includes a tiny, barely recognizable Perel brother in the background). While Wall was making his kind of work, Leo was carving away in obscurity, creating an outsider's art in the heart of the West End. Past these holdouts from a vanished city wandered an ever-shrinking, nearly invisible population of aimless men and women.

The West End has become too expensive to continue as a kind of *de facto* retirement village; when I lived there it was full of elderly ladies— holdouts from a more tranquil, Victorian time of tea and cakes—walking their poodles and pulling their shopping home in little metal carts on rubber wheels. The area had its share too of aging men who had been loggers or worked in the shipyards that have more or less disappeared from the city's inner harbours. These men rented rooms in the big old mansions that had been converted into rooming houses. One tenant rented what had been the mahogany-trimmed dining room, another got the sunroom with papered-over windows and more camped out in the dingy bedrooms.

A few of these hard-up men still make their rounds. You see them first thing in the morning, rubbing their necks, barely awake, making their way along the sidewalk to no particular place. I think of them as a kind of ruined army crawling out of their trenches—rooms full of empty tins, old newspapers piled against the walls—to make a pathetic assault in an effort to retake their turf. Each morning, they re-enter the newfangled city of boutiques and tailored blossoms, a city of many currencies and *haute couture,* of designer kayaks. They must feel like aliens, these men, who've been transported against their will to an unknown place where the air renders them invisible. After coffee and a couple of cigarettes they manage to dig out of their pockets, and a few deep breaths of that old sweet air, do they crawl back to their rooms, lie down in their cave of a bed and think they dreamed everything that buzzes and jumps outside their greasy windows?

Like the dwindling contingent of seemingly aimless men, there are still a few hundred (could there be more?) old buildings that have somehow escaped the wrecker's ball and stand as unchanged mementoes of the West End's early years. These are rambling two- and three-storey, clapboard and shingle places, windows blocked with tinfoil, boards loose on the stairs, dank air lingering in the hallway behind the front door. Standing in the yards of these old houses are forlorn-looking cloth-seated lawn chairs, beaten thin from being left out in the rain; little piles of tools, tins, work gloves and unrecognizable oddities that make up the materials of an eccentric tenant's gardening habits. You have to be a bit of an eccentric yourself to love these places, with their jumble of peaks, dormer windows, little bottles lined up on sills, haphazard fencing, additions and fire escapes tacked on as successive generations try to remake buildings constructed for very different kinds of people into something they themselves can live in.

I talk with artist Michael Kluckner, who has a stake in the city's bohemian heritage. Kluckner found himself painting the buildings that had been designated for destruction in Vancouver's downtown. His subjects include neighbourhood houses and apartment blocks, but he has also done portraits of the single-room-only hotels along West Pender, the neon nights of Hastings.

Kluckner lived in the West End for more than a decade, beginning in the 1970s. His books, including the lavishly illustrated *Vanishing Vancouver*, pair his subtle watercolours with detailed stories connected with each location depicted in his paintings. The elegance, along with the melancholic nostalgia that characterizes Kluckner's work, has helped bring attention to the preservation of historic sites. I took *Vanishing Vancouver* with me when I left the city, partly because of the image on its cover, which reproduces an evocative painting of the Gainsborough Apartments, where I lived alongside the rambling stucco rooming house where Leo rented his room and kept his studio. In Kluckner's painting, two walkers carry shopping bags in each hand. The hawthorn trees are bare, but there is a great deal of green in the stands of cedar and holly. From the angle Kluckner chose, the front of Leo's house blocks the view of the second-floor window that was my living room. In *Vanishing Vancouver*, Kluckner asks quite sensibly if a "restored" house worth saving as Vancouver heritage is one with all its architectural accretions removed—all the additions and changes wrought by one generation after another—or if it isn't truer to the life of a downtown Vancouver building to look overgrown, tumbledown and eccentric.

Kluckner is about a decade older than I am, but those years give him the important edge of having lived in the West End at its most carnivalesque, at a time I paradoxically think of as being its glory days. Still, I'm anxious as I head to meet him because what he has to tell me of West End life in the 1970s may have little to do with my fantasy of a balmy Pacific decade of ease and love. Kluckner's paintings preserve the memory of the kind of West End street that had lots of room for men like Leo and my younger self. I arrange to visit him to find out what he thought the city has lost along with the disappearance of the often humble structures his paintings portray.

Today, Kluckner lives with his wife on a farm in Langley, minutes from the American border. Called Killara Farm, his property is a long drive out of the city, first south along Oak Street to Highway 99, where an exit just short of the U.S. boarder takes you east, beyond the rural intersection of 8th Avenue and 216th Street, through which the locals are just as likely to pass on horseback, white-hatted, as in their cars or trucks. Tin mail boxes on wooden poles mark each front gate, and the properties are much deeper than they are wide. I'm close enough to the American side that some of the backyards I pass may easily back onto Washington State. The sun is high and hot. I'm early for our appointment, so I drive past Kluckner's gate and park in the sun, where the road dead ends. On the radio Bob Dylan's "Positively 4th Street" broadcasts its odd, misanthropic message: "Do you take me for such a fool to think that I'd make contact? You see me on the street you always act surprised."

When I get out of the car, the dry ground crackles with grasshoppers, and moths flap by sluggishly. The Canadian sky is perfectly blue; it seems to have depth and texture, like a glass bowl full of water. On the American side things look less dramatic, more burned out and pale, with tattered clouds trailing above the trees in the southern distance. Leaves come down from a stand of birch along the roadside, each leaf hitting the gravel quietly.

At noon I nose the car up against Kluckner's gate and get out. Beyond it I pass the rather desperate-looking but elaborate rose garden that Kluckner's wife has tended against all odds on these low, hot flatlands. As Kluckner walks toward me, he's followed by a wayward crew of white chickens who look a bit like a comic version of a successful man's bodyguards. The man they appear to guard looks much as he might have—with an additional touch of grey—when he returned to Vancouver from San Francisco in high hippie style, driving a Volkswagen station wagon with everything he owned in the back. Kluckner is tall and lean. He wears his curly hair long and his beard is neatly trimmed. He shows me around his studio, a low building with southern exposure built onto the side of his house. As we settle down on kitchen chairs to talk, I watch the browned-out grass blowing beyond the window in the late-summer breeze.

The first thing Kluckner recalls about the West End in the 1970s has to do with the rather menacing way landlords dealt with the tangled zoning laws that prevented them from developing their properties.

"The old houses would burn routinely," he says. "There was always one around the corner going up, and no one had called the fire department. Certainly not the landlord. You know, there was better things he had in mind for the little piece of property under his old cottage."

Kluckner admits that there are aspects of the major changes that swept though the West End over the past twenty-five years that lent the neighbourhood new energy and even made it more liveable.

"It's true, the old rooming houses were torn down. These buildings—great old stone mansions built by rich men, with their beautiful craftsmanship—were disappearing to make way for massive apartment buildings. But that development, in theory, was providing housing for many, many more people. Giving them modern housing. And this would be for a pool of office workers who would live within walking distance or a twenty-five cent bus ride from downtown. Compare this to the model that took hold in Toronto in the 1960s. Since then, there's been too little affordable housing downtown, and people have to come in from Markham and Brampton, and they hate each other by the time they get to work."

When I first lived in the West End in the 1980s, a cap had been placed on building and population growth in the area. The outcome was that it wasn't easy to find an apartment, but the streets were stable and no one was being pushed out as higher priced residences replaced affordable rentals.

"The early seventies and even into the eighties were a great time in the West End," Kluckner says. "There were so many streets where there were just a ton of people and relatively few cars. But that profile, which was true in other neighbourhoods like Kitsilano, began to change drastically in the late eighties. That was when we witnessed an historical first. For the first time people were tearing down really nice houses and trees, only to replace them with houses. So it suddenly became more clearly a conservation issue and an environmental issue and a character issue. I thought, before too much time went by, all these buildings that I was painting would come down. Partly, I was painting them because I knew them. But you could have arrived in Vancouver in early 1988 and experienced old Vancouver, whereas if you arrived in 1990, it was all gone, you know. It was ripped up. This isn't completely true, but you could walk down a street and just everything was changing so fast. And not in the way the West End had changed in the 1970s, with more people moving in. Now, the West End is changing back, because a lot of the walk-up apartments, the 1950s apartments, have been taken down. Even the more substantial 1930s buildings, but they're being replaced by buildings like Eugenia Place next to the Sylvia Hotel, which is one suite per floor. And a lot of those are held by off-shore people, so on that site I'll bet you at one time there aren't more than twenty people. I know the people who have the twelfth floor there. They're acquaintances of my wife. They have a very wealthy son who bought them the suite so they could have a nice old age."

Although I've admired Eugenia Place, a sleek concrete and glass condominium that replaced a modest mock-Tudor apartment block (which in turn replaced wooden beach cottages), I have never seen anyone enter or leave through its front door. The building, which faces English Bay, is one of the more dramatic projects of Vancouver architect Richard Henriquez, whose designs, rather ironically in light of Kluckner's point, always tell a story about the structures his buildings supplant.

"I know Richard," Kluckner says. "I like his designs, and I like the stories that lay behind them. But a building like Eugenia Place contributes to the depopulation of the West End. That's a key concern now, I think." Interrupting himself, Kluckner points to the card I'm carrying with his painting of the Gainsborough and the two old houses to the west of it. "In my time and in your time in the West End, in those two houses there were tons of people. That's what made the area so fascinating. And when you look at the way some of the old houses are renovated as condominiums, they're so bloated, full of people's stuff. There isn't room for many people with all the stuff they've got inside. I would, if I were king, put a ceiling on the number of square feet of each individual suite built. So there wouldn't be any one-suite per floor buildings. You could do a pocket—call it the Gold Coast—around English Bay. The rich people

*West Coast folk art with
a bohemian touch*

could have that. But put a ceiling elsewhere at, say, fifteen hundred square feet or two thousand square feet in order to keep the population density."

Kluckner's ideas sound sensible to me. They don't preclude development. They even offer the most extravagantly gorgeous views to those who can pay the highest price for them. But they are also in favour of maintaining the variety and sheer numbers of people that always made the West End an exciting place to live.

"Vancouver has still got some pretty significant public space that is very beautiful," Kluckner adds. "English Bay along the sweep of the beach there is just a magnificent place. The Sylvia Bar is still good. The way the wind blows in from the west, the nice sea breeze, and the way the sun goes down, with people out on the promenade. Given that socially we're not at all like the people who laid out these beaches and walks—it's amazing we're even the same species if you talk about public behaviour and dress— it's just astonishing that that design works so well for contemporary people, an absolute triumph of some kind of universal urban design."

A place where the inhabitants of a Canadian Gold Coast might rub shoulders with Leo as he trolled English Bay, hunting up driftwood for his next project. This sounds like a worthy goal to me. Utopian you say? After I say goodbye to Michael Kluckner, I cruise back downtown to meet a friend for dinner, and end up parking not far from Leo's place on Broughton Street. I take my camera along and am not surprised to find a particularly lively display on show behind the holly bushes that stand between Leo's yard and the roadway. Just above the shrubbery I can see the upper half of two hand-carved, brightly painted figures, a man and a woman almost to full scale. There is something Teuton or Swiss about their heads, their square-jawed faces framed by braided, cinnamon-coloured hair. The female figure balances a yellow crescent moon on her head, using one hand to hold it in place, and in the moon's concave middle sits a pink infant, waving his hands and feet. The male figure uses the top of his head and both hands to support a big-cheeked, satisfied-looking sun, which has blue eyes and cherubic red lips. Attached to this sculpture—clearly Leo's latest—is a "For Sale" sign with a phone number. I find myself hoping that those Gold Coasters need a bit of folk art to go with their million dollar view.

A recent show at the Or Gallery, provocatively called "Heart of Darkness," will in fact be the last in the old Perel Brothers building, since the gallery's board has decided to leave Hastings Street for a more visitor-friendly part of the downtown. "Heart of Darkness" is not just art on walls; it's bait set out to tempt the upstanding people of Vancouver to come and view the work of B.C. culture heroes Emily Carr and Jack Shadbolt in the black hole of Vancouver. When I drive down to the gallery late one night with Reid Shier, just before the show is to open, he laughs as we pull up to the curb, recognizing the interest our car will draw from late-night wanderers. Sure enough, as we climbed out onto the street corner, a loose gathering of salesmen shoulder toward us calling, "Hey, my friend . . . do you wanna . . . how about a bit of . . ." The come-ons are a latter-day version of the voices who called out to my great-uncle as he opened his shop. The voices are soft but insistent. Their offers go unanswered as we walk past them into the night.

What Lies Below

PEOPLE ON THE WEST COAST of Canada think of the great cedar forests as remnants of an eternal landscape, the last vestiges of an otherwise vanished primeval country, though it's worth remembering that the great ranges of the northwest coast are a climax forest, the last stage of an ever-changing cycle of growth. Dwellers on the Atlantic coast are hard-pressed to find a similar natural shrine to venerate. The European need for New World timber was so great that vast tracts were deforested long before much of what would become Canada was settled. The trees of Newfoundland and New Brunswick were prized by French and British shipbuilders as masts. Around Fredericton an entire white pine forest was felled for this industry. But this transformation above ground is overshadowed today by changes beneath the Atlantic. The ocean, people fear, has reached a climax of its own, an end to the fish stocks that maritimers have long thought of as their share of an eternal bounty, the East Coast version of a primeval landscape. The inhabitants of Newfoundland's outports, settlements as old as any European-settled town sites on the continent, can do little more than wait and see if the ocean has truly reached a climax or if there are further surprises in store for those whose lives rely on what's hidden in the sea.

I visited the Maritimes for the first time to give a paper at the annual Learneds Conference, the kind of gathering of Canadian university teachers and writers that newspaper columnists love to make fun of by listing the most outlandishly titled conference papers. The conference was in St. John's—not Saint John, New Brunswick, where they like both words spelled out, but St. John's, Newfoundland. A mysterious place to non-Maritimers. A kind of country within a country, I'd heard native Newfoundlanders say. Growing up in Calgary, I knew nothing about Newfoundland but Newfie jokes, which seem to have run their course. I also knew that when the economy was good on the prairies, many Newfoundlanders were drawn, against their will, to well-paying Alberta jobs.

One thing central to life in Newfoundland that we've all heard something about is the cod. The cod are not where they should be. They've gone. It's still an open question where they went to and whether they'll come back, but one thing we do know for certain is that they have not been hanging around Carbonear or Trinity or English Harbour or Bauline or Portugal Cove, and they have not been farther out to sea, where the large offshore trawlers have been taking ton after ton for decades. In the 1570s, when English fishing boats came from Poole to the summer fishing grounds on the banks of Newfoundland's Trinity Bay, sailors could almost rake the cod in the way a kid nets goldfish in a bowl. Did the fish go up the spout of some ingenious Basque fishing vacuum wielded from just inside international waters? Were they over-fished by the Newfoundland coastal fishery, who were fed over-optimistic forecasts by government experts? And who was to blame for these? Did the scientists get things dead wrong, or were their warnings simply ignored by government bureaucrats eager to please constituents in an era when politicians are held in lower esteem than ocean bottom feeders? What does a fishing family do in the spring and summer when the fish just aren't out there to go catch? How would a British Columbian feel if he woke up one morning and heard the news that the last load of timber had just been trucked to the coast for pulping?

There wasn't much talk at the Learneds Conference about the cod stocks, though I did chat with a few hungry delegates about where in St.

John's we might dine on the much-ballyhooed local delicacy: cod tongues. These, strangely, were on every menu, regardless of the crisis in stocks at sea. I was biding my time till later in the week, when I had plans to drive north along the coast to see Trinity, one of the many old fishing outports that line the province's coves and harbours. It was at these outports that modern Canada got its start, where Europeans began to settle in numbers after years of simply harvesting the fish and then heading home. Trinity, it's said, is the oldest European settlement on the continent.

IN THE DAYS before heading up-island, whenever I have a few hours free from conference-going, I set out on the half-hour walk from Memorial University campus to downtown St. John's and the harbour. The best route seems to be along a street called Newtown, which could be a road in half the neighbourhoods in the country. Post-war bungalows sit on weedy lawns, and I don't bump into a soul. Cars are pulled up on driveways, and angry dogs bark from behind high fences. Rounding the hill that separates the campus from the downtown, I pass a cemetery whose gates hang crookedly, while half its monuments tip at crazy angles. White plaster angels point their snub noses at the ground. I wonder why the families these tombs belong to don't come out one afternoon and do something about gravity's insult to their dearly departed. But then, maybe death doesn't have to be tidy in St. John's. As I walk down the road on the back side of the hill the old town comes into view, looking a bit like Penzance, the English coastal city St. John's is twinned with.

Considering its age—St. John's was established in the seventeenth century—the city lacks the character and coherent style of an old English coastal city. Five fires during the 1800s destroyed substantial portions of the downtown, and the streets above the harbour have a picked-apart look. But there is something distinctly Canadian about this too. So many of our medium-sized cities and towns share the same dispiriting jumble of new and derelict buildings, shiny government and bank outposts looming over great, unrentable heritage blocks.

Regardless of how strongly the locals feel that their island harbours a culture different from the rest of the country, St. John's, at first glance, doesn't strike a visitor as being that different from, say, Yorkton, Saskatchewan, or Lethbridge, Alberta. Subtract the harbour and what have you got? A place that probably looked better fifty years ago than it does today. In St. John's the teenagers are lean and straight-haired, the expensive restaurants serve undercooked potatoes and there's one new, bunkerlike expensive hotel in town, where the clients move with a look of self-satisfaction, a bit like winter grouse do as they march along a garden wall, sunning themselves on a bright afternoon. If you wander around long enough you can find a place that serves a decent piece of carrot cake, and in the centre of the city, you will come across an impressive-looking war memorial that is easily the best landscaped piece of real estate in the city. In St. John's the war dead are treated to a good view and the nicest garden. But what does a visitor see in St. John's that he's not seen before? The wooden houses piled on top of one another on the hill above the harbour, the steep lanes and stairways threading between them; a stone church on an untended plateau of grass and leafless trees, across from a huge parking lot, which is the most haunted-looking building in town, after the old gothic Masonic Lodge.

On a sunny Friday morning, St. John's streets are quiet, with the odd office type on her way with a brief case under her arm. The light on the pavement and the sky and the general emptiness on a workday morning remind me of the Sunday quiet of Calgary in the 1970s, when trains blocked traffic at level crossings and the trees gathered the city back into their shade, beckoning with a wave of their arms, the green gum of their leaves.

I find a pub that's worth searching out on Water Street. It is, in fact, a little above the street on a lane that runs steeply up a set of cracked concrete steps. The Ship Inn resembles an English ale house of the early century. It was established in 1977, but the low-beamed ceiling, the dim plaster on the walls, the open iron stove burning one of those store-bought logs, the impractically small bar behind which one woman tries to serve drinks and food seem, at least in an urban Canadian context, eternal. The bar menu is slim: pies (salmon, chicken, beef, black bean), salads and soup. But this is Monday, which seems to account for the fact that there is no soup, no salad and only three salmon pies left. A number of the beers on tap are not pouring—their spigots produce foam and more foam, and then an inch or so of beer. But the woman behind the bar is so cheerfully unapologetic about all this that it is impossible to be anything but cheerful as you wait fifteen or twenty minutes to order a drink, chatting with the person standing beside you, who watches forlornly as another pint of foam is drawn.

The night's entertainment at the Ship Inn turns out to be a play with at least ten actors called *The Skinhead Hamlet,* whose main innovation, aside from it's shortness, is that every character's favourite word is *fuck.* This makes the show sound more like a Canadian Student's Residence Hamlet than anything else. But the actors are having a lot of fun, so the crowd in the bar does too. Throughout the rest of the country, people are in front of their TVs watching the federal election results roll in with a certain grim expectancy. And our obliviousness to this at the Ship Inn, along with the raucous play, the rambling conversation in front of the bar, the aimlessness of waiting an hour for a salmon pie, creates an unusual feeling of community in the room. The ale house is its own parliament of carousing locals and conference-goers, student actors, with one upbeat golden labrador for variety.

I plan to leave for Trinity the next morning, and as I come out of the Ship Inn, onto the steps that led up from Water Street, there is a thin mean rain falling. It is June and almost cold enough to snow. The sign outside the bar looks very old, much older than the pub, as if it had been nabbed at the closing sale of some Dickensian London ale house. It shows a ship with billowing blue sails full of bitter wind making its way against an apocalyptic-looking yellow sky. As the ship wavers in the grey lamp light, I think of the Rock, as Newfoundland is called, likewise holding out against rough seas.

TRINITY IS LOCATED on the eastern end of the Bonavista Peninsula, one of the land masses that juts into the Atlantic on the eastern edge of

Downtown St. John's

Newfoundland. Trinity harbour is itself a gathering of outcroppings that push like spread fingers into Trinity Bay, which creates the snug gathering of points and coves that gave the harbour its reputation among early European fleets as the best cod-fishing grounds in the world. The harbour's twenty-one miles of shoreline offered shelter for hundreds of vessels to summer as their crews worked. The English fishing boats came for seals and salmon, but it was cod, dried and salted on wooden platforms, or cod liver oil that became the real economic draw. The vessels would arrive in the spring, fish throughout the summer, and leave in late September. For more than three hundred years, Trinity was cod heaven to a prospering British migratory fishing fleet. Gradually, a more settled population took root. By the mid-1800s, Trinity was a sizeable outport.

When I call around to Trinity's inns and bed and breakfasts, I find that I'm not the only refugee from the St. John's conference who wants to visit the eastern outports. Every available room in Trinity is booked. Finally, an English-accented voice at the Village Inn tells me it has a room. So off I go into the early June cold in a rented car so clean it squeaks in the rain.

Some people like the worry-free newness of rental cars, but I prefer driving trips that start from home in my own car, a twenty-eight-year-old convertible. It's noisy on the highway, with the wind rushing in where the top fastens to the windshield, making it difficult to listen to the radio. Bits of road grit and the odd bug make their way in where the weather stripping has dried and shrunk. And depending on your politics, you could say that my gas mileage is either a joke or a crime.

But adventuring in a rental car is like going out dressed in someone else's clothes. As soon as I start out along the section of Trans-Canada that skirts a bluff across the harbour from St. John's, I begin to notice all the other identical rented Pontiacs and Chevrolets trailing me, and I can't help feeling that I've linked up with a club, like the Airstream trailer troupes of the 1950s, whose key urge was to take all the comforts of home with them as they convoyed through the Arizona desert.

In the old convertible back home, I may look like some drop-out from a Jean-Luc Godard film or an overgrown kid who can't let go of the kind of car his father loved to drive, but at least I can feel the road under the wheels of the car, and I don't have to worry about a lawsuit if I spill coffee on the seat between my legs. When the original pioneers struck out for the coast did they go in someone else's boots? Did they ride a squeaky clean horse they'd never seen before? No, they didn't. They looked at their sad old nag, wondered if she'd make one more long haul and took their chances.

Many of the drivers in this anonymous fleet of rental cars rolling forth on a cold, codless afternoon have undoubtedly been drawn by the tourist events planned by the province at Bonavista, the town where, legend has it, Europeans first laid eyes on the maritime riches of this "new founde land." It's believed that in 1497, a few miles beyond Trinity at Cape Bonavista, the Italian John Cabot, sailing with the support of British investors, made landfall.

I am swimming in the current hype surrounding the anniversary of Cabot's arrival. The province's tourism industry has staked everything on this unique event. The Queen is due to do a float-about on board the *HMCS St. John's*, and a handmade replica of Cabot's caravel, the *Matthew*, is tacking treacherously from Bristol, England, where Cabot began his voyage. It is due to land at Bonavista on June 24 and then at sixteen other ports of call, of which the last will be Trinity on August 8.

I am nonplussed at first as I travel the strip of highway that curves southwest then northward from St. John's and skirts the bottom of Conception Bay. Coastal roads put me in the mood for the awesome sweep and softness of beaches on the West Coast. And as I head up the Bonavista Peninsula, the landscape bears some similarity to parts of central Vancouver Island; I get the same feeling of being up close to the sky as the roadway tops hill after hill. Lakes nestle against a rough shoreline, pines growing almost to the waterside. But here there is a foot or two of dead wood and rotted grass at the lakes' edge, where the frigid water stunts anything that tries to grow.

The road is wet with fog, the heavy air steel grey where it hangs in low valleys. I run through little fishing towns. Melrose. Port Union. Catalina. Little Catalina. The Trans-Canada bisects them: heading north on the highway the older parts of town fall away on the right, clustered around the coves. The oldest houses are four-square wood-frame buildings with ancient-looking curtains hanging in the windows. These buildings are symmetrical, two stories tall, with a slightly peaked roof, the door centred in the front wall with pairs of windows, one for each floor, looking like blank eyes. Often the houses perch precariously on a cove's rocky hillside. Some are painted bright colours—white with yellow trim, orange and green—but on many only a trace of their last paint job remains, and I can see almost down to the grain in bare boards that were milled generations ago. Around the old towns, trees are scarce, more or less obliterated to make way for settlement as they were used to build the houses themselves, for boat building or firewood. What shelter the landscape might have once offered inhabitants is gone, and the wind blows fiercely off the rough bay waters.

The impact of the weather here surely sets the eastern coast apart from the rest of the country. Here alone (aside from the country's northern territories), there is no summer when you might expect it, very little prospect of sunlight and fog that makes the day seem as though it must struggle to establish itself. A shadow of mist threatens to hang forever over the roadway.

These coastal towns I pss through all seem to have two churches, often a big Anglican one dwarfing a Catholic or Methodist competitor across the street, the way competing gas stations face off from opposing corners in the city. Some towns have a Masonic Lodge, some an Oddfellows Temple. Elderly couples walk along the roadside, taking their daily constitutional, and pairs of women in track suits march to the IGA. The best-kept building is usually the postal outlet, or, if the town has one, the government building. Road crews lay down new blacktop or regrade the shoulder of the main road. Everyone seems to have a great deal of firewood laid up, cut, not as it's done out west, in triangular wedges, but in lengths chopped from the full diameter of the tree. Wherever I go, an advertisement follows me on the car radio: a chorus of chipper voices singing about the shish-ke-bob at some local restaurant.

Just as I begin to think I know what a Newfoundland outport has to offer, I arrive at Trinity. The town site sits on a tongue of land sticking out between two encircling peninsular arms that block a view of clear ocean. I approach the town on a road that skirts the rocks high above Trinity harbour. Little piers poke out into the water, and from the road I look down at houses that seem to hang precariously from the rock.

I stop the car on a hill of wild grass and rust-coloured lichen and look down at a village of red and green-roofed frame houses. Brick chimneys poke above the roof lines. Two church spires are the town's skyscrapers, one a rather modest bell tower fastened to the front of a white-painted box of a sanctuary, the other a prouder red tower capped by a clock and a cross that sits at the top of its fluted peak.

The inner harbour is boatless. Wooden piers jut into the slate-grey water, and a load of firewood is neatly piled on the gravel just up from the

Trinity, with its enclosed harbour, seen from the roadside approaching it

shoreline. Smoke puffs from a corrugated metal shed, where someone must be at work, but there is no one in sight.

I wind my way down the hill into town and follow the white-picket-fenced roads to the Village Inn. The inn turns out to be one of the bigger buildings in town, bigger than the neighbouring houses, smaller than the church with the clock tower and the parish hall, and smaller than the buildings that housed the Ryan Premises, a fish wholesaling outfit that once had offices in the most productive Newfoundland outports. Cars look out of place on Trinity's single-lane roads, as if they've landed from another planet. And the little collection of visitors' rental cars looks particularly goofy in the inn's modest lot. Pulled up tight to the side of the building is a grey Zodiac boat hitched to a trailer.

Although Trinity looks like an interesting relic—a Canadian version of the well-preserved colonial main streets of the American northeast—I have only an inkling upon arriving that it has anything to offer beyond its history. At first glance it seems to have nothing but history. Modern conveniences—cars, electricity, a sharp new post office—have seemingly been grafted onto a museum of a place. I find myself thinking of Poe's murderer bricking his cat up behind the basement wall along with the fresh corpse of his wife. If I knock against one of Trinity's old walls will I hear a faint, terrified *meow?*

In the churchyard there are grizzled gravestones leaning tipsily this way and that, the once-elegant script on their faces blasted off by a few hundred years of winter wind. The local museum might be the town's own tombstone. Located in a converted house across from the big church, it showcases mementoes of busted booms, of a doomed economy, of wartime patriotism and royalist enthusiasms. The museum's collection includes old planes, saws, typewriters, sewing machines, buttons, hair combs, photos of the town girl guides, dentist's equipment, eyeglasses, sleds, barrels, military uniforms in transparent suit bags, Coke bottles, tobacco pouches, model ships, rug-hooked decorative pictures under glass, portraits of Queen Victoria, scythes, cook pots, scales, a spinning wheel, lengths of rope tied in reef knots, shoemaker's tools, equipment for a game of nine pins, ladies' skates, circa 1910, a pair of knee-high sealskin boots, men's spats, brass door knockers, snowshoes made of boards, a chart with details of the Jewels of the Masonic Lodge, big iron door locks, wooden rifles, two needlefish lying at the bottom of a jar in a few inches of green water, a box for holding minister's collars, one-hundred-year-old silk dresses, calipers used to measure a ship's mast, a squid pounder, a glass float of ghostly green used to keep fishing nets on the water's surface, harpoons for spearing tuna or pothead, a three-fingered iron prong for digging potatoes, kerosene oil lamps with fluted glass cases, a seal club, a policeman's truncheon, a mug commemorating the coronation of George VI, a twelve-pound cannonball, a brass hot water bottle, plates of whale baleen that look as elegant on the wall as a Japanese fan. All of this, amazingly, was once commonplace. Everyone in Trinity has one or two of most everything housed in the museum's cramped rooms. But now it is all like the leftovers of another world. Jules Verne stuff.

Doorway in Trinity's churchyard

The woman minding the museum wears her coat inside and coughs a rough smoker's cough when she isn't yawning and looking out the window at what is, I imagine, her house across the street. At the back of the museum's yard there is a pair of his and her outhouses with a sign on the door telling visitors not to put paper down the toilets.

But as I soon find out, there is nothing antiquated about the goings on at the Village Inn. Things there quickly take on a strange forward momentum that I can barely keep up with. I am checked in by Christine and Peter Beamish, who own the inn. They are in their mid- to late forties, friendly, willing to chat. Peter is thick around the middle, sporting a bristling grey beard, and there is a good deal of humour in his eyes. He wears beat-up dock shoes, a loose flannel shirt and jeans, the gear of a fisherman ready to putter around on his boat.

When Christine hears my name, she remembers that when I called to ask if there was room at the inn, I'd mentioned my plan to hunt up a story about the town.

"Got any ideas?" I ask as a joke, and she gives me the look this line usually gets. "You're the writer," she says. "You're supposed to come up with the ideas."

But Peter looks at me over his glasses and says he thinks he might have a story I'd like to hear.

I tell Peter I'd be glad to talk, though I don't yet know about what, and ask when would be a handy time for him.

"How about right now?" he says.

Christine offers to show me my room, and I promise to be right back down. We go upstairs and down a long hall to the back of the inn. The bed in my room is one of those Victorian models, strung high on springs like a trampoline, so you could easily pull a chair alongside it and use it as a desk. Out the window is a view of a red wood-frame house with mansard windows, and another wooden house that is boarded up. Beyond them is the grey water of Trinity Bay.

I gather my pen, notebook and tape recorder and come back down to the inn's front hall. From there Beamish leads me into his living room, which looks out over the veranda at the road. I sit on a long brown sofa while Beamish sinks into an armchair. Behind him is an upright piano with elaborate carvings above the keys. On the walls hang photos of whales breaching, whales slapping their scythe-shaped tails on the surface of the harbour, boatfuls of brightly dressed men, women and children watching the curved spine of a humpback as it rests at the surface of the water. On the mantle is a plate of baleen, once prized in the heyday of whaling as a flexible and sturdy substance the Victorians used for making whips, skirt hoops, umbrellas, corset stays and fishing rods. Whales, as it turns out, are Beamish's passion, but more directly he wants to talk about his experiments into the possibility of developing a coded language with which we might communicate with whales.

"We're gathering so much information from them," he tells me. "Since we stopped killing them, they've paid us back a great reward."

Trinity, according to Beamish, is the best place in the world to study whales. A number of species enter the bay in early June, heading north to feed on capelin, a herringlike fish that spawns in colder waters. The number of whales is increasing every year, and this season ten to twelve thousand fin whales, roughly fifteen hundred minke and eight hundred and fifty humpbacks will make their way north until December, when they turn around and head for warmer waters north of Puerto Rico to begin calving. Generations ago, Trinity was a good place to go if you wanted to kill whales. A whale factory was set up at the turn of the century, some three hundred yards upwind of the town at a spot called Maggoty Cove. As blubber was boiled to render the valuable oil, a pungent odour, to put it lightly, blanketed the town.

Beamish is a prodigious talker on subjects other than whales as well. These include everything from quantum mechanics to cod fish. And they keep coming up, those elusive cod, because Beamish has his own theory about why they're gone.

PETER BEAMISH came to Trinity twenty-some years ago from the West Coast, where he did a Ph.D. at the University of British Columbia. His research in Newfoundland began with seemingly mundane questions: how the humpbacks and other great whales use sonar to find fish. But his interests moved in a more unusual direction as he picked up on research being done by scientists in Russia into the way foxes and eagles communicate with each another.

"What the Russians were interested in," he says, "was how animals could survive and evolve using the few signals they had, signals being the sounds which make up an animal's vocabulary. Wolves, it seems, have 125 different signals they communicate with. I'd been studying the humpbacks here, and I'd found that they had about 140 different signals."

Beamish's communication research experiments consist of boating out into Trinity harbour in a craft outfitted with sound transmitters.

"Now, please don't say Peter talks to whales," Beamish insists. "Because it sounds bad and whales don't talk. No animals talk. But things work like this: the boat is outfitted with underwater sound transmitters. We go out every day and try to find out more about the elaborate communication system used by the whales. I can tell you that this system is far greater than the 140 signals that we originally knew of. Now we're estimating that the humpbacks can make use of tens of thousands of concepts when they want to communicate with one another or us. But to be able to communicate with them, we've had to create an artificial language where we define what our standard code will be."

It's not particularly easy for the layperson to understand how Beamish's code works. But the key to it is that animals—woefully short on vocal signals—have a way of making up for this weakness. And this has to do with the intervals, or rhythms, they use to vary the signals they send. Whales send signals in a number of ways, from breaching, flippering and blowing underwater to acoustic signals sent by way of high pressure air forced through valves.

"Say we leave the dock on a particular day at four," Beamish continues, "and we begin transmitting a signal with the big pinger every two minutes. We chose the two-minute interval because that's about the mean diving time for a whale. It can hold its breath a little longer or a little shorter, and it won't cause it any stress."

Beamish explains that the two-minute diving pattern represents the whale's deeper body rhythm.

"Think of your heartbeat: ba dump, ba dump, ba dump. It's much faster, but it's the same sort of thing. A biological clock. And when it's at its most regular and even, that means your body is under very little stress. Now the whale always stays twenty-five or fifty metres from the boat, blowing and giving signals at a range that he's comfortable with. Whatever keeps the stress low. And it recognizes our two-minute signals."

Exactly on the two-minute beat, Beamish explains, the humpback will slap its tail or leap or blow through its spout hole.

"A concept," he says, "is some information flow between you and the whale. The concept in this case is the two-minute interval."

To establish an artificial code between his signals and that of the whales, Beamish followed the example of his Russian counterparts and varied the signals his pinger transmitted.

"We would send a signal on time—on the two-minute mark—on time again, and then late by thirty seconds. Or we might send our signal late and late again by thirty seconds and then on time. Now we've done this twenty thousand times. The whale recognizes the change in interval. He's recognized the two-minute interval, and he recognizes when you're late. We established the combination of signals that goes out late, late and on time as a form of greeting. So we broadcast our two late signals, and we can count down the time until the third signal, which we'll send out on time—on the standard two-minute interval." Beamish holds up a photograph of a whale breaching, jumping straight out of the harbour.

"So I know how long I've got before that third signal is expected by the whale. I get a fellow to put a wide-angle lens on his camera. I move the boat very slowly around. And these four pictures illustrate what we call dancing—having these conversations. The whale has been listening to us. And he's recognized our two late signals, the intervals we've transmitted at. This creates our communication system. We watch the clock—five, four, three, two and boom—at the two-minute interval she jumps right on time." With this Beamish rises out of his chair and imitates the whooshing sound of a whale leaping upward from the bay.

I can follow this, the idea that a whale recognizes the intervals between a pulsating signal, but I can't guess what it is that would account for a whale getting involved in this sort of communication. What, I ask Beamish, is in it for the whale?

"First of all," Beamish tells me, "if a whale doesn't want to synchronize with our messages, he might just mill around; he might just want to look at us. But if he does mimic our messages back, he's usually overjoyed. The interpretation many of us have of this breaching—the question of why the whale jumps on time with our signal—is that the whale is elated, and possibly he has in his conscious mind the concept, 'Thank goodness you've discovered our way of communicating.' In other words, he's welcoming us into his world. And their world is altruistic, low stress, cooperative and based on rhythms, not on signals the way our high-stress world is."

WHEN BEAMISH AND I have spent an hour discussing his research, my tape recorder gives its familiar snap to signal that I am out of tape, which is not necessarily a bad thing. Beamish is so full of information that is new to me—some of it fascinating, some of it distressingly difficult—that I am literally swamped by the side issues he insists are intimately related to his communications research: Superstring Theory, Newtonian time, Steven Hawking's notion of a Final Theory for All Things. To most of us, this sort of stuff might as well be explained in Persian. It's not going to sink in. At one point during our long first talk, Beamish paused and said, "The last three or four minutes I've diverged from my major discovery (and I probably did it purposely) into three or four major fields, and I could go into religion as well or music. But that's why I decided to write my next book, which is one hundred essays on the applications of rhythm-based communication. It's called the *New Logic of Nature.* It will deal with medicine, math, music, philosophy and all sorts of applications for people communicating with animals and plants."

I'm not sure what to say in response to this, so I let Beamish get back to work, and we agree to talk again.

Following our talk, I go for a walk around Trinity. I head up the hill behind the inn to try to photograph the town's brightly painted wood buildings—the two churches, the pumpkin-coloured Parish Hall, the houses once owned by fishing families and now made over as inns and bed and breakfasts. There's a mean mist blowing, which isn't heavy enough to get me wet, but reminds me of how cold your hands can get shovelling snow. My camera lens is soon spotted with mist, so I make my way back to the car.

I drive along the secondary road that links Trinity with the main highway and circle out to Trinity East, a newer, less picturesque settlement that sits across the cove from the original town site. There I find another little church, one-storey houses with cars out front and beaten-up sheds beside piers that don't appear to be in use. Here, into the 1970s, another whale factory processed the slaughtered carcasses of minke and

English Harbour's pristine outport landscape

fin whales, and when it was closed, partly because of the international
pressure on Canada to stop harvesting whales, its Norwegian-born staff
joined Beamish's crew.

Farther along the coast road is the elegantly named outport of
English Harbour. There look to be about fifty houses in town, and the
road snakes along the edge of the cove below towering lichen-covered
cliffs. I pass a pier where there are no boats in the water. A lone man carries nets and buoys from a shed to the edge of the pier. Like a number of
routes I've travelled in Newfoundland, the tarmac gives way to gravel as
the road rises into the hills and lands me on top of a craggy outcropping
that looks back at the scattered homes of English Harbour. There is one
miraculously located house nearby, a modest bungalow with a movie-
quality view of unimpeded ocean from bluffs that rise hundreds of yards
above the water's surface. In many near-abandoned outports, this sort of
property can be had for what many people pay for a new car.

I continue along the edge of the bluff, but once I've travelled for half
an hour with no end in sight, I turn the car around and head back the way

I came. The view of grey-green rock cliffs and open ocean, of stones covered in lichen the colour of fall trees, makes me wonder why the people who run the tourist show around the *Matthew* didn't plan to land their replica of Cabot's ship at this magnificent place. Since there's no historical evidence that Cabot made landfall at Bonavista, the insistence on putting on the main tourist show there seems pointless. The focus of the Queen's visit—all her meetings with local politicians and media—will take place on a bare outcropping of rock where the wind does a good impression of thrown knives and there is nothing in sight but an old red and white lighthouse, a statue of John Cabot and a great deal of shiny new tarmac.

These oddities of Newfoundland tourism put me in mind of an e-mail a friend sent me after his visit to Trinity. Under the title "more words about missed opportunities" he wrote

> We did go to Trinity—both the historic place and the newer community—but somehow you must have been gone, Norm: it was a day later than you'd said you'd be there, but we looked anyway, and enjoyed the fitful sun and strolled around an archival kind of place, watching the water for mythical ships and wondering where tea shops might be, or decent craft shops—feeling like tourists and wanting to leave money behind in exchange for something, anything other than the paltry and twee goods on display in the so-called craft shop. It made me angry, thinking about all these people looking to turn their economies around by opening to tourists but not being guided adequately by any kind of ministry of tourism about how to do so. it was like ireland deja vu the late sixties and early seventies: heartbreakingly naive people desperate for cash and making fools of themselves in the process. Some Newfie joke, eh?

I hunt for a place to eat dinner in Bonavista but have no luck. Everything is closed or looks quite uninviting. I decide to try the dinner menu at the Village Inn. It turns out that the other guests have also taken the path of least resistance and come back for dinner. The dining room, with panelling on the walls and vinyl banquettes along one side of each table, looks a bit like the kitchen in a Swiss cottage. A drug rep from St. John's eats alone. A woman reads the *Globe and Mail* and keeps to herself. I recognize a young couple with their child whom I saw in St. John's at the Learneds Conference. He is an Anglican pastor from the University of Toronto at work on a biography of Bruce Cockburn. She is a religious studies professor. As the wait staff go about their work, Beamish serenades us on a little accordion. When he takes a break from this, I eavesdrop as he chats with two young women at a neighbouring table. First they chat amiably about lichen. But communication with whales soon becomes the subject under discussion. Either the two women are asking better questions than I did, or Beamish has given them a better delivery, because I find his points clearer as he covers them with these two politely nodding guests.

It is at this point, as I finish my vegetarian chili and chat with the pastor from Toronto about the market possibilities for a Cockburn biography, that I realize that Beamish tells everyone who will listen about the theories his research have generated. It is his mission to do this: the inn is his church and we are an unsuspecting congregation. As Beamish explains the system of intervals he uses to query the whales on such subjects as their preference for dining on inshore capelin or offshore capelin, one of the women takes a final bite of her dinner and asks, "How do you know they're not just humouring you?" I admire the pluck of this, and Beamish takes it in stride. He's a believer. The unfaithful don't worry him. He has infinite patience for the cynicism of city slickers.

After dinner Beamish announces he'd like us to see a film about his work. It's shown on one of those old classroom screens that is unspooled with some difficulty like a Marx Brothers prop. The familiar, now antique click-clack of 16mm film threading through the projector accompanies images of Beamish out on his Zodiac, sometimes seeming to float close enough to the massive resting whales that he could reach out and touch

The Ryan premises on Trinity harbour

the arch of their back. The film offers a far lighter and more layman-friendly version of Beamish's research. It focuses on the more touristy whale-watching charters that Beamish mans when he's not building up rapport with the harbour's humpbacks.

As the film ends, the door of the inn opens and another familiar face appears, asking a little worriedly if there's a room left at the inn. The late-comer is another conference-goer who's driven up from St. John's, a man I know from Vancouver, where he teaches at U.B.C. Tony joins the rest of us in the inn's front room, looking a bit corralled and very much like he wants a room, maybe a drink, but definitely not a focus session. The conversation soon comes around to the question of how animals communicate with one another and with us. Beamish and the young couple from Toronto discuss what our host calls animal altruism. He has colourful examples of the way species help each other find food and play together. Beamish has a charming and intimate way of describing the way fish will switch positions to knock food into each other's mouths, the way a school of humpbacks will gather under a group of dolphins and shoot water through their blow-holes so the dolphins can gleefully ride the jets like a water slide. To make his idea of altruism as concrete as he can, he even describes a hypothetical exchange between whales and dolphins.

"An animal will actually do things for another animal without any requirement of an immediate reward," Beamish explains. "Say a group of humpback whales heading for the Strait of Belle Isle meets a group of dolphins. Making use of their one hundred and some signals the dolphins will have what we call a conversation with the humpbacks that goes like this: 'We're hungry,' the dolphins will say. 'We've come five hundred miles and haven't found anything to eat.' 'Well,' the humpbacks will respond, 'we passed five tons of herring a couple miles back.' 'A-ha, say the dolphins,' and off they go."

I'm quite taken by Beamish's loving descriptions of the daily life of animals. He has a knack for mimicking the way a whale uses its flippers to feed or the way an unusual sea bird will puff out its breast. His love of whales and his belief in the ecological lessons we can learn by entering into their rhythms, into what he sees as the potential for harmonious existence, is uplifting. His outlook is so utterly removed from city life and from most people's daily ambitions that I have trouble imagining Beamish at his physicists' conferences in Manhattan, navigating the traffic of a cosmopolis, where altruism is in short supply. You could say that by trying to introduce us to his research and its outcome, he is presenting us with the possibility of a new Canada, one whose rhythms are based on a different idea of communication and an unusual partnership among species.

With their two-year-old in bed, the young Toronto couple let themselves sink into Beamish's big, brown sofa. They respond with patient interest to the difficulty and, at times, the oddness of our host's ideas. They seem intrigued by his scientific proofs of a kind of afterlife, which has to do with the way cellular energy slows down to a point where it can reintegrate with the natural rhythms around us. The Torontonians appear amused, even a bit troubled, as Beamish rises to what he admits is his most operatic condition of science fictional propositions, in an effort to elaborate his idea that the rhythms he's recognized in the communication, diving and feeding patterns of whales are part of a pan-natural body of rhythms that all creatures—human, animal, vegetable, even mineral—can merge with. When we die, he hypothesizes, our rhythm—be it a heartbeat or the constant motion of waves along the rungs of our DNA molecules—slows down to that of wood or earth. This explains, he says, how what we call the "energy" or "information" in our DNA molecules can be reintegrated with the larger scheme of things. Making use of an anecdote that hovers somewhere between scientific proposition and religious parable, Beamish suggests that the dead may be all around us. If after her husband's death, a woman sees a white starling at a regular hour every morning for a week, she might have been visited by the energy of her absent beloved, which is still contained and circulating in the surrounding landscape.

Tony, the latecomer from St. John's, catches my eye and we agree on a visit to a pub called Rucky's, which is a few short blocks away. But Beamish has moved on to the subject of the cod's disappearance, and I convince Tony to stick it out a bit longer. On this subject Beamish is confidently single-minded. There's nothing apocalyptic about his view, and there's room in it for government error but no large-scale conspiracies on the part of federal or foreign powers.

"Between 1987 and 1991 there was an unusually cold August," he says, "that killed the inshore capelin. That's the fish that the cod feed on. And the cold came just as the capelin eggs were hatching. That's how nature hit us here. The temperature was down for five years. So the cod starved to death. We know this happens every sixty or so years. A wobble in the earth's axis causes a jog in the ocean's currents that brings very cold streams up into our waters. You can count on it," Beamish says confidently. "A failure in the fishery every sixty years."

I am an attentive and open listener when Beamish and I are on our own. I take down what he says and store it away for later digestion. But on the way to Rucky's, I find myself following Tony's lead toward a skeptic's view of what we've heard. I think too of a friend's recollection of his years working for the Federal Fisheries and the overly optimistic cod stock forecasts that circulated in the mid-1980s. Over-fishing, my friend thought, based on these misguided predictions, had to be a part of the picture. He'd gone on to describe the awesome fishing power of the large offshore trawlers that have been in use during recent decades.

RUCKY'S IS SET UP for business in a makeshift building covered in aluminum siding, which houses a big, dark hall that seems an appropriate place for a bingo tournament or a bake sale. The patterned brown linoleum is worn before the bar, where six or eight local guys lean, drinking Black Horse and Hibernia, pushing their baseball caps back on their heads to look out into the dark room, then pulling them back down over their eyes as they turn back to their beer. In the corner on a little pool table under one of the room's only bright lights, a noisy ball-bouncing game is being played by two young women. They turn out to be part of a theatre troupe touring the province in a production based on the story of the Viking arrival on the Newfoundland coast about one thousand years ago. This is another only partly verifiable event, like Cabot's landfall, but the story plays a powerful role in the island's sense of its past. The women in the group are Newfoundlanders, but they have no accent I can hear, as if their term at the National Theatre School in Montréal has trained it out of them. I'm no good at guessing ages—they might be eighteen or twenty-five—but they have that uncommon actor's poise; they sit with backs straight as they chat, and they speak without the *you knows* and *uhms* that most of us rely on in conversations with strangers. They turn up their faces, framed in the darkened room by long hair, as we talk. I wonder to myself where they hide this poise when they play Viking women, or did their parts call for an uncommon self-possession?

In the corner of the bar, three men huddle around the kind of video slot machines you find in pubs and grocery stores, dropping Loonies like they're garbage. I notice that Peter Beamish has come in. He doesn't approach us at first, but he doesn't exactly land anywhere else, and I can't help wondering if he's come to talk more about his beloved whales. But

A shed on the shoreline of Trinity Bay

instead he motions to the slot machines at the back of the bar and says that a local doctor lost ten thousand dollars on one of them. Then he says good night and heads off into the dark, where the actors hover with their pool cues slung like six guns at their hip.

Leaving Rucky's we step out onto one of Trinity's uncanny streetscapes in which twentieth-century men and women walk down eighteenth-century streets with corners akimbo, knee-high picket fences, neatly maintained frame houses with lace window curtains, a deep fog drifting over everything and illuminated by porch lights, the small islands of grass bearing no similarity at all to suburban yards. The spires of the churches hang in the fog as if we had stepped into a scene from Edgar Allen Poe. But the only animals out with us after midnight in Trinity are tomcats—grey, orange, white—turning this way and that on the lookout for uncovered garbage.

WHEN PETER BEAMISH takes his boatloads of tourists out for a look at the whales, it's the breach, the leap from the water and the great slap of the tail that everyone wants to see. But the real story at Trinity—at least for the last four hundred years—is not what goes on above the surface: the real action is hidden beneath the bay waters. Capelin. Cod. Minke whales trundling as far north as Labrador and then south again with the coming of cold. We no longer chase the humpback for its oil or the fat lodged in its skull. And with the voluminous undersea world of the cod fish in question, at least for the time being, Peter Beamish may be tuned to tomorrow's ocean, as he takes the measure of a whale's interest in us and enters the slow rhythm of conversation emanating from deep in Trinity Bay. In his way, he may have uncovered something for future dwellers at Trinity to stake their lives on, when the cod are no more than a detail in a story of the coastal life of long ago.

About the Author

PHOTO BY SHELLEY BUTLER

NORMAN RAVVIN grew up in Calgary and moved to Vancouver to study literature and history. He lived in Toronto for ten years, where he continued his studies, worked as a journalist, taught and wrote his first novel, *Cafe des Westens*, as well as his story collection, *Sex, Skyscrapers, and Standard Yiddish*. Both received critical acclaim. He also lived in Fredericton, where he taught creative writing and edited an anthology, *Great Stories of the Sea*. Norman Ravvin now lives in Montréal with his wife and new baby, where he continues to write and teach. His eclectic interests include vintage cars, jazz and travel. He is also the author of *A House of Words: Jewish Writing, Identity, and Memory* and a forthcoming novel, *Lola by Night*.